OUR IMPRISONMENTS

(Anger, Jealousy, Lust, Ego Attachment, Addiction, Fear & Greed)

I0201529

OUR IMPRISONMENTS

(Anger, Jealousy, Lust, Ego Attachment, Addiction, Fear & Greed)

By C.S.Bairagi

Charanjit Singh Bairagi

ISBN : 9788193160510

Published by Moksh Publications

"Liberation is your birthright and anything that feels like a prison, like a confinement, needs your attention."

CONTENTS

ACKNOWLEDGMENTS

I am deeply thankful to all the visible and invisible hands that have gone into the making of this book. Without their assistance and blessings I could not have done it. From the ones who inspired me to write to the one who has handed it to you, they all play a significant role in the manifestation of this work and have made it possible for me to reach out to you and share my being with you.

I am as grateful to those who have printed and distributed my work as I am to those who have earned for all of us the right to freedom of expression. There were days when it was not possible for an individual to speak the truth and share it with others. We are all very fortunate to be able to do so and should respect this freedom by not saying anything or writing anything that invades the space of others and hurts their sentiments. I therefore thank those who reviewed my work and provided me with a healthy feedback.

Even the tree, the wood of which the paper of this book is made from, deserves my thank you. We are all connected in a way that goes far beyond that which is obvious and we often fail to extend our gratitude to the silent existence that helps us realize our dreams. I thank everyone and everything responsible for all that I am and this book is a gift from me to mother-nature.

Introduction

Liberation is your birthright and anything that feels like a prison, like a confinement, needs your attention. Spiritualism is not very difficult to explain or understand. It is simply, freeing your soul of all imprisonments. It is, becoming aware of these sophisticated bars and then working your way out of them. It is being able to see the chains that are tied around the feet of your being and are making it tough for you to walk around. We have been living in these invisible jails for so long that they have become our homes. The world beyond our assumed limitations is unknown to us. Every now and then someone manages to jump across the high walls of the conditioning of the mind and enter the realm of enlightenment. But, the rest of us live and die within the four walls of mass consciousness.

To a bird in a cage the greatest gift you can give, as an expression of love and compassion, is to open the gates and let it fly back to the open and vast sky. That is exactly what I have tried to do. I have tried to assist the bird of your soul to fly out of the cage of spiritual enslavement. Watching that bird happily disappear into the vastness would be my joy. I love liberating and I love liberators. I write to liberate others and I liberate myself to be able to write about it. The freedom we have earned as nations is no doubt a great blessing. But it is only an environment. Authentic freedom has to come from within and only after having earned it can you call yourself a free man in a free country.

I have witnessed my near and dear ones go through great pain and suffering because of the control exercised by invisible forces like lust, anger, greed, attachment and ego over their soul. I have myself gone through an unbearable amount of it and would wish to eliminate as much of it as I can. It is quite tough to watch someone close to you consulting half a dozen doctors, spending thousands on clinical examinations and experimenting with 50 different medicines, never knowing that the real sickness is his or her ego. It is as if you were cursed to watch the whole drama helplessly. It is as if you know what someone is suffering from, have got the cure for it but can't give it because the one who is supposed to take it is not yet prepared to take it. It is a perfect situation for compassion to be born, a strange blending of helplessness, acceptance and understanding. The more I watch all this, the more I ponder into the potential of the various methods that can liberate a soul from its traps.

The forces we are dealing with are very powerful. Every spiritualist, sooner or later, finds himself standing in a Kurukshetra at the very spot where Arjun was standing in the battle of Mahabharata. Wherever you look, you see the sick and the suffering and the only space left for you to stand on is, surrender to and acceptance of, the form in which life has unfolded before you. The space is so thin that it feels as if you have nowhere to stand. This space has been described to be thinner than a hair and sharper than the blade of a sword. As far as I have come on this way, I perceive it as the space of the witness – the "Sakshi".

Liberation is for the freedom conscious; your freedom and the freedom of others. Anyone who has a vested interest in the dependence of others does not like the very idea of liberation. To him or her, it sounds like mutiny. What are martyrs for a country that is fighting for its liberty, are extremists for its rulers. One calls them, "Shaheeds", the other calls them outlaws. So, spiritual liberation is only for those who are highly conscious of the space that every soul needs to bloom. This space will not come from invading and conquering others; it will come from emptying yourself. The more you understand the distractions within, the more space you create for yourself and for those around you. In this space the greatest human virtues can come into being without any deliberate effort. The spiritual history testifies that.

Our soul has been captured by our mind and all that the mind is capable of creating. Getting it released from this captivity ought to be at the top of our priority list. All else should be secondary. The temptations of this world will stay but we won't. These lusts and greeds won't run out of stock but our incarnation will. The energy that we have got should not be spent on seeking pleasure and avoiding pain; it should be spent on transcending all such polarities that encourage dualism. If indulgence had an inherent potential of setting us free, all brothels would have become schools of enlightenment. But the only positive value of an indulgence is its capacity to make us realize that we can never have enough of it. And whether you indulge in food and sex or you indulge in anger and ego, they all work in the same fashion; they live through you. They use you as a vehicle. But you can use them as a vehicle instead. And that is exactly what I wish to share with you here.

In the process of reclaiming the lost kingdom of your "self", there will be many ups and downs, successes and failures, plateaus and slopes; you must not take them too seriously. Keep reminding yourself that it is just a process. You are not playing with toys here; you are working on invisible forces that have written down the history of mankind. Every now and then an anger, lust or ego will pin you to the ground the way a strong wrestler pins his opponent. You will be taken for a ride and you will lose a bout. But it is just another bout and one of the participants had to lose. No defeat is final; no failure is final. They are just a process. Hold on to persistence and your devotion shall be honored. God is on your side because you are reaching out for it. In the sacred books it is written that if you advance one step towards God, God advances twenty steps to receive you at the "Gates of heaven". May God bless you with total liberation and then assist you in liberating others.

Charanjit Singh

"Spiritualism is not about stuff that no one can understand; it is about doing something about the things that stand between you and your happiness."

Part I

Anger, Jealousy & Lust

Chapter 1 – ANGER

Just as we have two forms of water at high temperature – the hot water and the steam, similarly we have two major forms of anger that appear in us; the fire and the explosive. Up to a certain degree it exhibits itself in the form of a blaze and after that it becomes an explosion. The blaze burns everything; the explosion sends everything into splinters. As long as it can be controlled, it is a fire; but when it becomes uncontrollable it feels like a blast. In our modern world, it is one of the most frequently displayed emotions. Its tides rise and fall a dozen of times in us every day and yet we have never really tried to know what it is.

Anger is the most destructive of all the human emotions. Within seconds it can make someone commit a crime that can send him or her for a life imprisonment. Within seconds it can make you do something that turns your life in a totally different direction. I personally had a tough time riding this "Wild horse with no reins." My outbursts earned me a lot of negative publicity and people used to ask me with their looks, "What kind of a spiritualist are you? You have absolutely no control over your temper." And they were right. Critics are right a lot of times because a critic spends most of his time making sure that his point is valid. The ego is fiercely afraid of losing. So, my critics were right. I had absolutely no control over my temper. I was like a land mine. Here someone stepped on me; there I would blow off.

An angry man or woman is like a pressure cooker. Every now and then you hear a whistle or two and the pressure inside is building up most of the time. There are a thousand ways to build up that pressure. There are a thousand ways to push such emotional buttons. If we have no control over our self we have got the whole world to control it. Anger is, in fact the best thing to start from if you are serious about the realization of the self. Spiritualism is not about stuff that no one can understand; it is about doing something about the things that stand between you and your happiness. And who is not interested in being happy? So, you can start with anger if that happens to be your greatest problem. If it is lust, start with lust. Evolve the most natural way.

Now suppose someone gives me a call and abuses me on the phone, someone I don't even know. It will obviously make me explode. But let's examine the episode closely and find out what is going on behind the obvious. In this particular case, someone has invaded my birthrights with foul language. This invasion is a stimulus and my anger is my response to it. Every anger is a response to a stimulus. A sage observed that between a stimulus and our response to it, is a thin space and our destiny depends upon the choices we make in this space. I heard this in one of Dr. Deepak Chopra's talks and it really gave me the breakthrough I needed so badly. That observation is the key to unlocking the mystery of anger. This gap between a stimulus and a response is what we have got with us and we can use it to shape our world the way we would like it to be. Our life is going to be the decisions we make and the karma we do in this space.

When one ascetic's father died, his last words to his dear son were, "Every time someone provokes you into anger, postpone your response by 24 hours". If those were a parent's last words to a child, they must be the juice of his wisdom; they must be the essence of all that he knew. And they are because they have the potential to expand the thin space between a stimulus and the response to it. When an anger is diluted, it becomes less dangerous. What is anger today can become wisdom by tomorrow, if allowed to mature. But if expressed, anger is like a bullet that has been fired. It has its own consequences which are beyond our control. We are the masters of that bullet only as long as we have not pulled the trigger. We are the masters of our anger only as long as we have not expressed it.

Dr. Wayne Dyer uses the example of an orange. He says that when an orange is squeezed, what comes out of it is always orange juice; irrespective of who squeezes it and when. It is never an apple juice. And what comes out of it is what is inside. In the same way, what comes out of us when we are squeezed is what is inside us. If anger comes out of us then that is what we have got inside. The external stimulus merely stirs the water. If it becomes muddy by the stirring, the mud was there at the bottom of it. A woman can stir up the mud of lust, an enemy can stir the mud of hatred and a professional rival can stir up the mud of jealousy. The mud was there at the bottom of our consciousness. They have only stirred it up and brought it to our notice. We should be grateful to them for reminding us that there is still some work to do as far as the refinement of our soul is concerned.

The first challenge in case of anger is to avoid expressing it on the other. The second challenge is to avoid expressing it on yourself because that could make you a masochist, a self torturer. An anger that is produced because of an injustice of a very high magnitude is very difficult to dissolve; for example, the anger of a martyr, a freedom fighter or a revolutionary. So, if you can neither express it on the other or yourself nor dissolve it, then what can you do? You can use it to go beyond it. You can use anger to go beyond anger just the way you use the mind to go beyond the mind in Gyan Yoga. We all know that meditation can take us beyond the mind. But the other side of that coin is that without the mind we cannot even decide to meditate. So, whatever we have got, can be used as a vehicle to touch higher levels of awareness. And we have to start with what we have got. Where else could you start from?

Now lets' see how we can use our anger as a vehicle for evolving. Whenever anger shows up, pull yourself away from it and start watching it. It won't be as easy as it sounds. But then, we are not here to discuss easy things. Start watching your anger. Identify yourself as the witness to that anger. Don't identify yourself as the angry one. When your witnessing has developed to a considerable level, you will be able to see that anger is not alone, it has got an ego supporting it and backing it up. You will be able to feel anger as a dense cloud of vibrations powerful enough to make your body tremble. These vibrations have a numbing effect on your senses, your reasoning and your logic. They can totally overpower your being and take control of it if there is no one to witness them. The development of the witness is the secret to transcending your fury.

Usually, we become aware of our anger days after it has shown up. We look back at an event and say, "Oh, I should not have done that; I should have controlled myself". We are separated from our anger by the dimension of time. It can be good for a critical analysis of yourself but not good enough to transcend anger. To transcend it, you should be able to distance yourself from it right in the moment when it shows up. You should be able to look at it right when it is there in your body. When you do so, you are not separated from it by the dimension of time but by the dimension of awareness. You are not analyzing a yesterday; you are witnessing the, "Now", the very moment you are living. Once you have succeeded in doing this, all that is left to do is adding strength to the witness and making it powerful enough to stand on its own. It must not get carried away by the emotional tornadoes.

It is very important for us to realize that the losing of temper exhibits lack of control. Controlling others requires force but controlling yourself requires strength. I have often seen people with absolutely no strength of character trying to dominate and control others. I can see the futility of the whole thing. If there is something worth dominating and controlling, I think it is our own ego. So, we need to practice control over our self. You can start with your eating habits. You can start from anywhere. It will all come to the same point. My personnel observation has been that almost all ill-health is because of lack of knowledge about foods and drinks and lack of control over your urges. I realized this fact when I listened to the talks of Dr. Pratap Chauhan of the Jiva Ayurveda organization at Faridabad. I must admit that his wisdom saved my life. He is really doing a noble job by living the disciplines of Ayurveda and sharing his insight with others.

Now lets' go back to anger. Whenever we deal with an ailment we have to consider two aspects of it; the immediate relief and the permanent cure. Anger is also an ailment. Dealing with it when it is generated is an immediate relief while finding where it is coming from and then doing something about it is the permanent cure. As far as I can see, I think the anger generated in us is not totally because of a particular incident; we have got a lot of residual anger in us. All the unexpressed anger gets deposited in our soul and erupts like a volcano at the slightest provocation. You will often find people astonished at your response to provoking incidents because your anger won't be directly proportional to the weightage of the incident. Even your opponents will feel that you are over exaggerating things and blowing them out of proportion. Their observation is correct. Your residual anger has got added to the incidental one.

Residual anger can be dissolved with dynamic meditation designed by Acharya Rajneesh, massage, Pranayam, laughing and forgiveness. Massage releases the emotions that have deposited in our muscle tissues and layered there. Dynamic meditation does the same on the level of vibrations. So, you can say that it is a kind of spiritual massage. Pranayam or breathing exercises are for balancing our ethereal body and forgiveness heals the emotional wounds of the past. Laughing can assist you in replacing unhealthy thought patterns with healthier ones. You can device your own unique methods to get rid of residual anger and be fresh like a child once again. Residual anger is the actual disease; the anger in daily life is merely a symptom. It is just the excess that has poured out of our soul. The vessel of our soul is always filled with what flows out of it. Compassion flows out of a saint and anger flows out of an angry man.

There are some foods and drinks that generate aggression. Caffeine is one of them. White sugar is another. You can make your own list and then cut them down to healthy amounts. Loud, rock music with fast rhythms is also not a good diet for your ears to feed upon. It makes you aggressive. Anger always rides fast rhythms. If you are suffering from hypertension, then anger is one of its most prominent symptoms. Ailments like acidity and gastric problems can also easily make you angry. What I am trying to say here is that if the cause of your anger is a physical problem or a chemical intake, it should be dealt with, on that level. We are not here just to produce anger and then watch it. We are here to get rid of its excess in every possible way.

Anger has its own purpose. When birthrights of the innocent and the weak are trampled upon, anger is required to restore the balance. No battle for righteousness could have been fought without anger. But all these martyrs, revolutionaries and freedom fighters do not have anger in their hearts. In their heart, there is compassion. Anger is only on the periphery of their soul. It is not the driving force. Martyrs die and kill also but they never do so with violence and hatred in their heart. Their anger cannot be compared to the anger of a terrorist or a serial killer. They use anger for their purpose and they are able to do so because they have transcended anger. You realize the significance of the force of anger only after going beyond it. Not until then. If I were to sum it up, I would say that in the hands of compassion, even a sword can be a blessing whereas in the hands of anger, even a religious book can be a curse.

As long as you are kind to the kind and unkind to the unkind, you have not yet mastered your fury. And to be kind to the unkind you have to look at an ordinary situation in an extraordinary way. Lao Tse says, "What is a good man but a bad man's teacher and what is a bad man but a good man's job." You have to see every bad man as a good man's job. You have to give this old world a new meaning. I have come across drunkards at every stage of my life. The meaning of their existence has changed for me with every passing decade. We cannot change situations but we can surely change the meaning we give to them. It is one way of interpreting Dr. Wayne Dyer's words that when you change the way you look at things, the things you look at, change. Anger can be dissolved in its origin if we change the meaning we give to the very situations that make us lose our temper. One way of doing that is by looking at your incarnation with God's eyes every time your patience is put to test by someone.

When someone deliberately disrespects you and pushes you where it hurts the most, you are in for a real spiritual test. If you allow your consciousness to get entangled in the chemistry of a painful relationship, it can prove to be a great challenge. You have to separate your karma from the karma of others. This separation could be your breakthrough. If someone is being rude, that is their karma; if you are being kind, it is your karma. Don't be tolerant. Be kind. Tolerance sounds like suppressing your anger whereas kind indicates the total absence of anger. Let your acts be totally independent in their nature. They must not be reactions to the karma of others. If someone has chosen to walk the path of an ego – they have chosen to spend their incarnation that way. Allow them. Save yours and chose to spend your incarnation on the good of all. After we have run out of our lifelines, we will all have to go back to our source and on that last journey our only luggage will be our karma – good or bad. So why not spend the limited amount of breaths we have got in a wise way instead of just throwing them around foolishly.

"As you sow, so shall you reap" – Those are not just empty words put together to make a sentence; they are the juice of all the incarnations we have lived so far. We have been sowing unconsciously and reaping unconsciously. Now is the time to sow consciously and reap consciously. Our deeds, our karma are the seeds and our soul is the soil we have got. Whether you like to hear it or not whatever you are reaping today, you have sown in the past. But the shift can be made in a moment. You can choose the seeds of compassion, gratitude, religiousness, faithfulness, tolerance, patience and service instead of hatred, revenge, jealousy and the like. Within six months you will be able to see your crop dancing with the breeze and your life moving in a different direction. So if someone is sowing hatred by treating you badly, there is no need to sow anger in your soul as a response to it. You can sow forgiveness; you can sow compassion. You must choose the seeds carefully to reap the kind of life you desire.

The line of demarcation between your karma and the karma of the other is the key to spiritual liberty. But it is so subtle that to see it you have to become as subtle as the line itself. Just the way you need an ear to listen and a tongue to taste, you need a high degree of awareness to see the subtlety of our incarnation. When you realize that we are all living in parallel and no one is accountable for someone else's karma, you cannot play the blame game anymore and you feel totally responsible for your deeds. You can see how a reactive mind traps all of us into karmic chain reactions and keeps us rooted in the mundane realities of life. Going into the depth of the causes of your anger can reveal great secrets. Instead of looking at anger as a problem or a challenge, you can look at it as a gateway to the great understanding.

When someone's behavior makes you angry, he or she has succeeded, at least in that moment, in pulling you down to his or her level of consciousness. If someone throws a stone at you and it hits you, you must be standing on the same ground as him or her. If you are in an aero plane, stones hurled at you from the ground cannot reach you. And that is exactly what saints are, they are people living on a very high plane of consciousness. The taunts and criticism thrown at them by the world do not hit their being. They have accepted the difference between their knowing and the world's ignorance and integrated these two realities in the designing of their life. They have mastered the art of living and sharing compassion while following the pattern of this world.

Anger is a disappointment. It is the difference between the treatment you expected from a person and the treatment you got from him or her. Where there is no expectation, there is no disappointment. When a dog barks at us, we are not disappointed because we don't expect anything else from a dog. But when we are abused by a man or a woman, it makes us angry. If we can accept people the way they are, renounce the ambition of reforming them and choose to be an instrument of God's will, we can be much more compassionate and much more efficient. If someone wishes to evolve and thinks that I can help him or her in doing so I should assist. But if someone wants to stay the way he or she is, who am I to make changes in God's creation and try to reform this existence? The man who has accepted disgrace cannot be insulted. The man who has no lust for a victory cannot be defeated. Throw away expectations and you have thrown away disappointments.

Whenever someone's karma brings you pain in any way, try to understand that it is all happening according to some divine law. The pain you are getting from someone is most probably the pain you have given to someone in this or a previous incarnation. In this perfect world, there are no mistakes. It has to be 100% precise. Even if it goes wrong by .0001 %, it cannot function. Your reactions can create more of that stuff. The way out is acceptance. It is the only way to get a "No objection" certificate from the divine laws. And acceptance comes from understanding. Understanding can dispel anger the way a torch dispels darkness.

Many a times our anger fails to see the whole of a person and is a result of incomplete knowing. If you knew that the teenager who is disrespecting you in some way lost his father a few months ago, is struggling with drug addiction and is going to die 3 years later, would you still be mad at him? We often get caught up in the density of an incident and are unable to take an aerial view of things. Our compassion is handicapped by lack of knowing and we respond to the provocations of others like an echo. Our anger is very natural, but it is immature. There is no mystery in it. And mystery is the fragrance of wisdom.

Now, here are some first aids for anger. It is a good practice to avoid conversations when you are angry. Anger can easily convert itself into words and pour out of your mouth. Verbal assaults are almost as destructive for situations and relationships as physical assaults. The moment you become aware of your anger, move away from others for a while and take an aerial view of the episode. Remind yourself that we are all guests on this planet with a return ticket. Even before we realize, the journey is over and it's time to report back to our source. If someone is unable to see that truth, take it as divine will and allow them to learn the lessons of life in their own way. It is not in your capacity to bring about a mass enlightenment. People you love will die, people you love will suffer. They will refuse to see what you see and chose to suffer. Love them anyway and defuse your anger.

Another good spiritual practice is to anticipate a confrontation and then steer the situation in the direction of peace. Anger never strikes like a lightening; it always builds up. If we stop feeding it with thoughts of aggression and don't add our energy to it, we can make it subside. Do it a few dozen times and you will be much better in handling your anger. Before I had started working seriously on my temper, I used to find myself frequently possessed by anger the way someone is possessed by a ghost. It would enter and exit my soul like a twister and leave me gathering pieces of its side effects. But now, I can see it walking towards me and trying to take me for a ride. It is an unwelcome guest. I know it will stay with me for a while. I allow it to stay and patiently wait for it to go. It takes its own time and then leaves. "See you again", it says when I leave it at the gates of my soul...... I know it will come back; sooner or later.

Our soul is like a vessel. You cannot keep it empty. You cannot make a vacuum out of it. You can only choose what to fill it with. A container that appears to be empty is actually filled with air. When we don't fill the vessel of our soul with love, forgiveness, gratitude and compassion, it automatically gets filled with jealousy, anger, lust, ego and all such negativities. You can either spend your incarnation trying to throw these "Darknesses" out or you can bring the lamp of love into your soul. The most effective way to invite good emotions into your soul is by getting up early in the morning, having a full body bath including your hair (Kesi-Ishnaan) and reciting God's name of your choice for an hour or two. This technique has a great hidden potential to get you in touch with the dimension of love. A day begun in this way has far more chances to be spent in a positive manner. The first thousand thoughts of our mind can decide the flow of our day and it is easy to tap positive emotions when there is no traffic of thought vibrations in the ethers.

It is very essential for you to know that a judging and criticizing mind is very easy to provoke into anger. When judging and criticizing becomes your habit, you are always looking for faults and weaknesses in the personality of others. Your attention adds energy to things you don't want in people and they start behaving exactly the way you don't want them to. You never realize that it is actually your judging mind that is blowing things out of proportion.

If you start looking for the perfect man or the perfect woman, you may have to wait all your life and the day you do find one, you may realize how imperfect you yourself are. Too much of judgment and criticism in our mind can make us incapable of relating to anyone. No one wants to be judged and criticized. We all long for unconditional love. Therefore, do not judge and do not criticize and you will be less prone to the invasions of anger.

When you deal with people or when you live with them, they are going to make mistakes. It is just the way a child makes mistakes when learning how to write. We don't start beating up a kid because of a spelling error. People are just grown up kids. It is almost impossible for them to do something without making a mistake. You will have to create space in your consciousness for their errors and allow life to unfold the most natural way. Your anger could actually be an interference in the natural flow of things. When you are pushed; bend. When you are criticized; listen to the healthy part of it. When you are cheated; forgive. When you are disrespected; remain kind and when you are hurt, heal yourself with love. The negativity of this world has got a gravitational pull of its own that can keep your consciousness on the ground. To overcome that pull, you will require the wings of love. The more you use them, the stronger they will become.

I have enjoyed the company of saints and one of the things that attracted me in the first place was the absence of anger in their being. There was something in their presence that said, "I am free of the stimuli of this world." The vibrations of someone who lives beyond the lusts and greeds of the world are a rare phenomenon. They baptize your soul. The truth is that if you have found a saint, you will soon find God. You rarely find a saint losing his temper. Their compassion has got a base with such a large surface area that the pushes of this world are unable to throw it into an imbalance. Even when they are angry, there is compassion behind it. Their anger is like the slap of a parent; it is for the overall good of the child. Sitting close to a saint is like sitting by the side of a lake and throwing small pebbles into it. The ripples disappear; the serenity enters your soul. Being in the presence of and observing the liberated can be a great tool in freeing yourself from things like anger. Moreover, it can give you an idea of the life that lies beyond all that you have lived so far. So, don't be angry; be wise. Be kind.

May God bless us all with compassion.

"No defeat is final; no failure is final. They are just a process. Hold on to persistence and your devotion shall be honored."

Chapter 2 – JEALOUSY

Poison can be kept in a bottle for a century. Unless someone consumes it, it is harmless. But jealousy, if kept in a human body for even a few years, can eat away that body, sicken that mind and weaken that soul. If I go to a clinical laboratory and get my blood tested, it won't show up in any of them. The physicians will only be able to see what it has done to me. The origin of all the physical and psychological deterioration will stay a mystery. Only a spiritualist will come to know about the poison that is consuming the bottle it is contained in.

If someone is jealous of me and I am not compassionate enough, my first reaction will be to hate that person for what he is. Now he was sick. And instead of giving him medicine I have given him another sickness. That is how these things grow and multiply. We ought to treat jealousy as any other ailment. It is a spiritual disease. A jealous man is a sick man. And the cure is compassion. Not only will it stop those chain reactions of destructive relationships, it can lay down the foundation stones of mass healing.

Wherever there is comparison and competition; there is jealousy. Nature knows nothing about it. A shrub is not jealous of the tree nearby, a rabbit is not jealous of an elephant, a sparrow is not jealous of an eagle and a rose is not jealous of a daffodil. They are all busy being what they are. They are neither "Inferiority complexed" nor "Superiority complexed." They are not more than or less than someone or something else. Their life is an absolute simplicity. No ambitions, no destination, no comparison, no competition. They contain the Sutra for a stress free existence. But we are too wise and too proud to learn from a blade of grass.

When we teach our kids to stand first in their class, we are teaching them to compare and compete. By coaxing them to be better than everyone else, we are breaking them away from humanity and isolating them. Soon they will be travelling alone on the deserted path of selfishness and lose all their divinity. On one hand they will be worshipping God; on the other hand they will be manipulating and exploiting fellow human beings. This basic split in our thinking is responsible for all the harm that one human being is doing to another. We need to educate our children in the virtues of sharing, compassion and oneness.

The jealousy of one can create obstacles in the path of the other. If I am putting 10% of my energy into making something happen and someone is putting 50% of his into not letting it happen, the results won't be very encouraging. Jealous people destroy themselves and do a lot of harm to others with their negative vibrations. Many of them fall in love with the destructive power of their mind and are stopped only by a life threatening consequence. They revise their thinking only when their very existence is threatened. Sometimes it takes more than one such incident to bring them back to their senses and make them realize that God does not encourage violence of any sort. Jealousy is nothing but a violence done with thoughts. Whether you kill someone with a sword or with your mind, it makes no difference. Violence is violence. A jealous person has, in a way, converted his mind into a knife and is committing crime without being labelled a criminal.

In the eyes of God, a jealous human being is like a cancer cell in a body. It is destroying itself, its fellow cells and the very body it is living in i.e. the existence. We are all connected in a very mysterious way. If I drop a stone on my foot I am bound to feel the pain; if I harm a fellow human being, I am bound to suffer. But when someone's jealousy has become chronic, he or she is unable to see the implications of such a thinking. I have often witnessed people laughing at the suffering and pain of others and many a times using it as a source of entertainment. Our ignorance has no limits. We often fail to see very simple facts. If jealousy is harming the person who is receiving it, how could it benefit the person it is emanating from? If a person is sending jealous thoughts to 10 people, each one of them is getting only 1/10th of the harm that such thoughts are doing to their producer. Where do you think all these tumors, ulcers and cancers come from? They are all a byproduct of negative thoughts directed towards others and towards ourselves. They are all a physical manifestation of a way of thinking that does not have compassion at its nucleus. When we move away from compassion, we move towards suffering and ill health. When we are rooted in compassion, we cannot harm the other.

History has witnessed the greatest of jealousies. Jesus was crucified because of jealousy. Socrates was poisoned by the jealous. Guru Arjun Dev Ji went through so many hardships because of the jealousy of his real brother Pirthi Chand. The Pandavs suffered so much because of a jealous cousin Duryodhan. Lovers like Heer-Ranjha, Sohni- Mahiwaal and Mirza Saheban could not live together because of someone's jealousy. This sickness is scattered all over the history of mankind. Like the thorns that come with a rose, a bunch of jealous beings are born the day a Messiah is incarnated. God blends together these opposites in a strange fashion and makes his mystery all the more mysterious. You cannot jump out of the equation between Yin and Yang without first choosing on which side of it you would like to be – the sacred or the evil. You can either be jealous or compassionate. You cannot be both. You cannot mix poison and nectar because a drop of poison could be enough for a gallon of nectar.

There are three major prerequisites for a jealousy to be born in a person. The first is that the person wants something; the second is that he or she doesn't have it and the third is that someone else has it. It could be anything; a child, money, success, fame, a life partner, material richness, power, a following of loyal disciples, faithful friends, health, beauty, happiness, talent or lifestyle. It could be anything that we can possibly desire. Unless and until we do something about these prerequisites, we cannot get rid of this sickness. Instead of cultivating a mind that is occupied with wants, we need to live with an attitude of gratitude. Instead of emphasizing on what we don't have, we need to emphasize on what we do have and expand it into "Enoughness." Instead of distancing ourselves from fellow human beings and making that separation concrete, we need to find joy in the joy of others and expand our heart in all directions to accommodate everyone.

I am absolutely sure about the kind of soul I am talking to. You are basically good. But while living in this sick world, you have picked up some of its infections and now you wish to get rid of them and detoxify yourself. Don't worry. I am here to assist you in this cleansing. I myself will be cleansed in the process of helping you. People like you and me are not comfortable with things like jealousy. We wish to dwell in the house of compassion. We know the taste of compassion but are unable to stay there. Our soul is pushed out of the circumference of love by the distractions of this world and jealousy is just one of these distractions. Jealousy is not our home. We would not even think about staying there all our lives. Our home is unconditional love. All we need to do is find our way back.

Let us first take a look at our wanting. Now, if I am hungry and I want food, I don't see anything wrong with it. But if my stomach is full and I want a desert, I have started moving in the direction of luxury. Luxury will be followed by greed. Someone rightly said, "God has everything for our need but nothing for our greed." Our desires are always overflowing. Most of them are not a necessity; they are simply a demand created by all the advertisements we see. The world and its temptations are always bombarding our mind and forcing it to want more. More......

more......more......more. The mind keeps on asking for more. It is like a well that has no bottom. You can throw the whole market into it; it will still keep on asking for more. So stop. Give your mind all its needs and a few of the luxuries and then tell it to stop asking for more. Remind your mind that you are the master and it is your slave.

The next thing to be taken care of is the "Not having" part of our wants. It is in fact the second half of our wanting. One half is asking for something, the other half is being fussy about not having it. Put together, they can rob you of all your peace. Again, advertising has a lot to do with it. Those ads make you feel as if you are depriving yourself of something you can't do without. Virtual necessities are created in your mind by the media. Assumed sources of happiness are painted for your innocent imagination and your subconscious mind is manipulated. Let us see what Lao Tse had to say about the craze of desires that tortures us. He says,

The five colors blind the eye.

The five tones deafen the ear.

The five flavors dull the taste.

Racing and hunting madden the mind.

Precious things lead one astray.

Therefore the sage is guided by what he feels and not by what he sees. He lets go of "That" and choose "This".

You should listen to Dr. Wayne Dyer's translation of Tao Te Ching if you wish to know more about the taste of the space in which Lao Tse lived. So, this "Not having" has to be replaced with gratitude for all that God has blessed you with. Just as we don't appreciate a cribbing family member or work associate, God also has no liking for a nagging human being.

The third constituent of a jealousy is, "Someone else has it". When we say someone else has it and I don't, we create a duality. We break existence into me and the other. A separation, a distance comes into being. It can take centuries for people to dissolve this separation. At the root of all hatred is this duality. What we need to realize is that we are different limbs of the same body. If the foot is massaged, the head is relaxed. If someone is happy and I am connected to him or her, that joy will become my experience also. But if I am rooted in duality, my happiness will always be relative. I will be happy when others are sad and sad when others are happy. My joy won't be a joy; it would be a comparative analysis. You need to jump out of your body and get into the person's who you are feeling jealous of. Go into the details of all the hard work he or she has done, the obstacles he or she has faced and the sacrifices he or she has made in order to achieve something that you want for yourself. Feel the human aspect of that person which is just the same as yours. Never feel jealous of a success; always be inspired by it. Don't be disheartened by the gap between where you are and where you would like to be. Take a closer look at your assets and you will find that you have got hidden treasures and invaluable blessings that went unnoticed due to your comparisons and competitions.

Now that we are familiar with the a, b, c of jealousy, let's see how we can totally eliminate this toxic waste from our soul. The simplest way I can think of is to recognize the vibrations of jealousy and the vibrations of compassion and then learn how to shift from the former to the later in the moment of its experience. The truth is that we have made that shift millions of times but we don't know how to. We don't know how to because we have never been a conscious witness of the shift. We were either a jealousy or a compassion; we were never ever a witness. We often spend a whole day in jealousy and then a whole day in compassion. Our moods are totally at the mercy of circumstances. Our mind is like a windmill; completely controlled by the winds of external stimuli. We often feel enslaved and possessed by our emotions. A mastery of our emotions is a must for stabilizing our compassion. The karma of others should not be able to topple our soul.

Every time you realize that jealousy has gripped your soul, think about the bigger picture of our incarnation. You don't even know if you and the person you are feeling jealous of will ever meet again or not. Maybe, you have already met him or her for the last time. The thread of life is so fragile; I have seen it snap so many times. We were born to coexist. There is no meaning in a life where two people live and die harming each other. Become aware of your own karma and refuse to be pulled into negativity by others. Refuse to step out of your house of compassion. If someone pays you a friendly visit, serve them with the best you have got, but if someone chooses to hate and suffer, allow them to be that way and move at their own pace towards purification.

Like any other ailment, jealousy can become chronic if not treated for very long. Our energy always flows towards the emotion that we are most used to. If someone has been jealous for twenty years, he or she is going to convert all the food he or she eats into jealousy. You can try to help the "Chronic Jealous" in a thousand ways; their immediate next karma will still be pure harm. All that you can do is pray for their wellbeing, love them from a distance, be compassionate and patiently wait for them to realize that they are themselves sponsoring their suffering with their ill intentions and making it very difficult for their well wishers to pull them out of their rut of negativity.

The combination of jealousy and intelligence can be a deadly one. If a jealous person is intelligent also, he or she can fire missiles of negativity from hundreds of kilometers and they will drop within the precision of a foot. The abuse of the mind is the greatest abuse on earth. Behind every hair-raising crime, you will find an intelligent mind that is cold and insensitive. People are totally unable to see that if God can allow them to be born and then feed them; he can also decide to demolish them. Our religions have always believed in the three facets of God; Brahma the creator, Vishnu the caretaker and Mahesh the destroyer. God offered us all his existence so that we could use it and enjoy. But most of us have abused everything and are therefore in pain and suffering. Intelligence is supposed to be used for the good of all life on earth; it is not for designing and focusing harms.

We all need to practice giving. Without giving, we can never know what it is to find joy in the joy of others and the wall of duality can never be dissolved. The more you give, the less jealous you will be. It is that simple. The more selfish you are, the more jealous you will be. Selfishness makes your soul shrink and become incapable of accommodating the other. And without accommodating the other, you can never get rid of jealousy. In the act of giving, your soul is extended and expanded. Even if you have got nothing else to give, you can still give something- you can forgive. Compassion does not require a palace with 500 rooms to live in; all it needs is a soul that knows how to give. If you have really discovered the essence of life, your first thought each day would be, "How can I give something to someone today."

Another remedy for the ailment of jealousy is accepting the uniqueness of our incarnation. We are all a product of our unique karma and there is no way you could compare one with the other. Comparisons are the breeding grounds of jealousy. If I don't have something and someone else has it, it is not that my share has travelled to him or that he has stolen my good luck or robbed me of my destiny. We are all directly connected to God. There are no intermediate souls to exploit us, control us and play with our destinies. I am exactly what I am supposed to be. You are exactly where you ought to be. We are all unique and that is the most beautiful truth about our existence on this planet. Comparisons simply do not make any sense at all. We are all a unique creation of the existence. The mysterious laws have blended together all our deeds, our karma and we are living the life we have designed for ourselves. If I am not happy with it I should work on improving it instead of comparing my haves and have-nots with those of someone else. My life, my death and my reincarnation - all are uniquely mine.

As long as you are within the reach of negative emotions like jealousy and hatred, you will have to deal with them on two different planes. You will have to be aware when they show up in you and be compassionate when they show up in others. It is easy to witness such flaws in others than it is to see them in ourselves. We are so close to them that we become one with them. The strategy in both the cases is almost the same with slight changes - it is, distancing yourself from the negativity and seeking refuge in the dimension of love. The mystery behind all this hide and seek is that just as a plane needs a ground to take off, our soul also needs repelling emotions to evolve. The treatment we get from the ordinary, pushes us towards the extraordinary. The suffering we get from our own negativity pushes us towards bliss. Though it is not an easy task but with God's blessings we can use jealousy as a tool to become aware of ourselves and the existence. A great physician can even use poison as a medicine. You too can use your spiritual ailments to measure your spirituality.

Our compassion is often put to test by the jealousy of others. How you respond to such provocations decides how capable you are in dealing with this sickness. It is easy to hate the jealous; it is tough to save that inner candle of love from blowing off. But if you pass the test, the rewards are worth the trial. The choice is always yours and your choice will decide whether you belong to the world of hatred or the world of compassion. This one choice could turn out to be the most important decision you have ever made, whether to make a contribution to the world of duality or to make a contribution to the world of love. These two worlds have always existed in parallel and you will most probably find them there every time you are born on this planet. So, choose compassion and then hold on to it.

Compassion is the greatest power on earth. It can immune you to the jealous assaults of those who are living on a lower level of awareness. Lao Tse says, "Respond intelligently even to unintelligent treatment." He is advising us to avoid confrontation and bend against the winds like a young plant. He is asking us to respond compassionately even to uncompassionate assaults. When you are rooted in love, you are rooted in God and the jealousies of men cannot harm a God. But when you step out of the dimension of love, you have stepped into the world and become a common man. So each day try to stay in the invisible space of compassion as much as you can. Just as our physical muscles are weakened if not used for too long, the invisible muscles of compassion are also weakened if we allow our soul to be rented by negative emotions. Strengthen these muscles with your Guru's blessings, meditation, selfless acts of giving, forgiveness and flexibility and avoid all foods and drinks that generate a lot of aggression. All the complications in our life can be simplified with the magic wand of compassion.

"Freedom is not the same thing as comfort. The distinction between these two ways of looking at life is very important to understand if you are seriously considering the option of salvation."

Chapter 3 – LUST

The word lust is used by many spiritualists to mean intense desire of any kind but for the sake of expressing myself, I am going to use it in context of sexual desire here. The life that God has designed for us to live is a strange combination of pains and pleasures. On one hand we have got pains like sickness, enmity, friction in relationships, poverty and death and on the other hand we have got the pleasures of the five senses, the pleasure of sleep, the pleasure of love and the pleasure of sex. As far as the magnitude of pleasure is concerned, lust is definitely on the top of the list and that is exactly what makes it so captivating for our soul. If someone wishes to transcend anger you can understand that. If someone wants to get rid of jealousy, you can understand that also. But when someone wants to transcend lust, only a few realize what that implies. Anger and jealousy are pains while lust is a pleasure. Well, it only appears to be a pleasure. Because a prison is a prison even if the bars are made from gold. Lust is a golden cage.

Unlike anger, attachment, greed, ego and jealousy, lust has a physical component also - the semen. So it is a very mysterious blending of that which can be seen and that which cannot be seen. As if this were not enough, there is yet one more surprise – its biological dimension. The magnetism of lust is born out of the forces of attraction between the polarities of opposite sex. You can call them the Yin and Yang or male and female. No matter what you call them, the spell they cast on the human species remains absolutely the same. To transcend lust, you would really have to be a spiritual Einstein. If there is anything more mysterious than lust, then it is either death or enlightenment. So, it is not without any reason that lust makes the whole world dance to its tunes. It derives its conquering ability from the magical making up of it. The common man does not seem to have any choice but to surrender to its prowess.

Anyone who wishes to master his lust is definitely declaring one thing – that he values his freedom more than his comfort. The distinction between these two ways of looking at life is very important to understand if you are seriously considering the option of salvation. Freedom is not the same thing as comfort. Our freedom fighters were not comfortable. They were hanged, exiled, drowned and blown with cannons. But they were free. In the very choice of accepting all the atrocities that came their way while fighting to liberate their motherland, they had liberated themselves. They had earned their freedom long before the nation earned it. For the common man, lust is a pleasure but for the one who has become aware of the way lust conquers our soul, it is something to be liberated from. This distinction is necessary because the one who cannot see a jail as a jail cannot be released from it.

Like anger, lust is also very powerful. It can make people jump into the filthiest of gutters once it has occupied the throne of their being. Lust gives a biological meaning to all the relationships of the one who is possessed by it. Things like loyalty, faithfulness, trustworthiness, honesty, chastity and innocence have no meaning for someone whose days and nights are charged with lust. It can swallow up all human virtues and reduce a soul to a hunger that can never be satisfied. For anyone who wishes to live a life of purity, an understanding of lust is a must. Because where there is lust, there can be no compassion.

First of all, let's see how much role our senses have to play in the mystery that surrounds the phenomenon of lust. Your libido can be triggered by looking at a nude picture, by listening to the voice of opposite sex, by smelling certain scents, by touching someone or even by thinking about the opposite sex. A stimulus can be sent inside your being from any of these doors. If there is no witness to guard these entrances, the thieves of temptations can easily steal away your conscience. A spiritualist must decide what to see and what not to, what to smell and what not to, what to touch and what not to, what to think about and what not to. These decisions are your karma and karma is all that you have got to earn a freedom. The purification of a soul is like the mining of gold. There is a lot of deliberate effort involved and a lot of processes you have to go through.

Now, the external stimulus is only a stimulus; the real thing is inside us. If, by chance a prostitute comes in contact with a saint what do you think her presence will trigger in him? Only compassion. Because, that is what he has got inside. He will not have lust for her body; he will have compassion for her soul and for her way of living. He will not see her as something to be used; he will see her as someone to be helped. Her body won't be a food for his sexual hunger; the saint will feel as if she is a temple that has been looted. The prostitute won't be able to pull down the saint; the saint may succeed in pulling her out of her dungeon. We often get so busy blaming the stimulus that the root of our problems never gets our attention. An enemy is outside but anger is always inside. Foods and drinks are outside but our eating habits are inside. Luxuries are outside but the greed and desire is inside. Arrogance and aggression is outside but the ego is inside. Similarly sexual stimulus is outside but the lust is inside.

Lust appears in the form of tides of pleasure and once triggered, it can stay with you even for the whole day, especially if it has something to do with your diet. So, that means you have got a whole day to study it provided you have the guts to. To study something, you need to keep it at an optimum distance from you, neither too close, nor too far. So keep your lust at an optimum distance from you. Don't feed it with your thoughts and don't add your energy to it. Like anger, lust also seeks an expression. But if you express it, you cannot study it. In the act of its expression, the witness is lost. When you become one with your lust, you have stepped out of the space of witnessing and offered both your mind as well as your soul in the service of your lust. But if you stay rooted in witnessing, the rising and falling tides of your libido will be absorbed by your soul and leave you intoxicated. If you give up and decide to go with your lust, wherever it takes you, you have definitely lost an opportunity to know it. Anyway, don't worry; it will be back within 24 hours.

What if you don't have any libido at all? Well, it can be even more threatening than having too much of it. For a healthy married life, an adequate amount of lust is essential in both the partners. So, you have to have it and have it under control. Though there are a lot of techniques to deal with lust but from my own experience I think the best way is to not add your mind and your energy to it. Treat it as if you treat someone who is neither a friend nor an enemy. If you make it your friend, it will start staying with you throughout the week; if you make it an enemy you will be busy throwing it out of your being. Just choose to be a neutral observer; neither entertain it nor try to get rid of it. Just watch it from a distance. Watch the crests and troughs of its waves. Notice how its intoxication tries to conquer the mind, the body and the soul. In the mind we have thoughts, in the body we have sexual organs and in the soul we have the witness. Like a clever politician, lust tries to win these one by one and add to itself. Each addition makes it stronger and thicker and also makes its victory more feasible.

Watching your lust and not allowing it to run its usual course will feel like renunciation. The pleasure is right in front of you but you are choosing not to have it. You may even question yourself, "What am I going to gain from holding myself back from a freely available pleasure that is my birthright?" Well, it is the price you pay for discovering the treasure of compassion. Your witnessing has the potential to convert all your lust into love. Our soul is a strange spiritual laboratory in which this can be evolved into that. The difference between lust and compassion is like the difference between an animal and a human being; lust belongs to a lower plane of consciousness while compassion belongs to a higher plane. If you wish to fly in the sky you have to leave the ground. If you cling to the ground, the sky remains unknown to you. Distancing yourself from your lust is just like lifting your feet off the ground. For a while it may feel awkward but the change will open up new possibilities for you. As far as I can see, witnessing is the best remedy for every spiritual plateau. Watching lifts you up.

The lust of a common man is a tussle between two extremities – the prostitute and the saint. The common man wishes to indulge like a prostitute and be free like a saint. Do you think it is possible? I don't think so. And the impossibility of it is his pain. Our relationship with our lust is a love – hate relationship. Sexual gratification requires the other and when you are dependent upon the other, you cannot be free. It is just like drug addiction. You want what the drug does to you but you don't want the drug. You find yourself caught up between two wants that cannot be fulfilled at the same time. Indulgence and freedom are like drinking and driving. The complexity of this situation can be simplified only by jumping out of the situation and looking back at the contradiction in your desires. It is as if we want to lose weight with a high calorie diet. Discipline is inevitable. There is no such thing as an "Indulgy Saint" or a "Saintly Indulger". The crossroads of life are those moments when God is asking you to make a decision and thus make a karmic investment. Life is a big Kurukshetra and there is an Arjun in all of us who is unable to decide.

Our lust is not something new. We have been living with it for, God knows, how many incarnations. In every incarnation, we must have danced to its tunes and fooled around on earth, living on chunks of life and trying to balance the equation between pain and pleasure. Our lust is not some discovery we have made; it is the work on ourselves that we have not done yet. Because of our lust, anger, greed, attachment and ego we have been sowing karma and reaping it. The poor soul has been a puppet since centuries. So, this is the moment for you to claim supreme consciousness and total liberty. Let your lust knock at the door of your soul for as long as it takes to make it realize that you are the master of your house. Let it go back disappointed and defeated. You have served it for long enough. Now let there be a reversal of roles.

The mass is living under the spell of lust because people are busy either denying and suppressing it or expressing it. No one is witnessing it. When you deny a truth, you end up living a lie. When you suppress a truth, it becomes volcanic. When you express a truth, you come to know about it and when you witness it, you are liberated from it. Lust is a truth and marriage is an arrangement for its controlled expression. A controlled expression saves you from a denial and a suppression of your libido but then it can get stuck at that level. Couples spend all their incarnation exploring all possibilities in sex and still end up knowing it only as a hunger that has to be satisfied. The space beyond lust remains unknown to them. They cannot even contemplate it.

Just as fasting makes you aware of your hunger but you end up thinking about food all day, celibacy makes you aware of your lust but you end up thinking about sex all day. The married know lust as a hunger; the celibate also knows it as a hunger. So how do you enter the realm where your lust doesn't ask for gratification, where it doesn't appear before you in the form of a hunger? As far as I can see, witnessing can be that breakthrough. Things like anger and lust are like ghosts; they can overpower us only as long as we cannot see them. When you can watch them paying you a visit, staying with you and leaving, you cannot be tortured. Marriage was not designed by our great ancestors for sexual indulgence; it was designed for understanding lust from a higher perspective and then putting it where it belongs.

In its healthiest form, lust serves two major purposes. There may be some subtle and sophisticated ways in which it moves pieces around but we shall talk about the two major ones. One is the reproduction of mankind and the other is the glimpse of enlightenment. God gave a moment of enlightenment to everyone in the form of the climax of lust. Though it is like a flash of lightening in the sky but that glimpse opens up the door to a realm of possibilities. Any intelligent man or woman can be convinced that if this much is there, there must be more. The climax of lust could be the climax of human consciousness. In fact, that was the basic truth behind Acharya Rajneesh's talks, "From sex to super-consciousness." But the mass has started gathering these glimpses instead of realizing that it is only a pointer towards a possibility; it is not the possibility itself. Nobody gets drunk with a spoon of wine even if you take one every few hours. A glimpse of a possibility is all that it is.

We carry with us, all our incarnations, things like hunger, sleep and lust but we never try to know what they are. These mysterious creations of God can be a ticket to liberation, if explored properly. We sleep every day, we eat every day and yet all that we know about them is that for hunger you need food and for sleep you need a bed. Our wisdom has only length and a breadth; there is no depth in it. Our wisdom of our lust is also very basic. And with a basic wisdom you can only live a basic life. You cannot fly with legs; you can only walk, jump or run with them. To fly, you need wings; the wings of imagination and awareness. An objective look at lust can be a way of developing these wings.

Three major levels come to our notice when we take an objective look at lust; the lust of an animal, the lust of a common man and the lust of an ascetic. At the animal level, its purpose is reproduction; at the level of a common man the purpose is reproduction and pleasure and at the level of an ascetic, its utility is evolution. The ascetic contains the lower two levels. He can use his lust to reproduce, he can use it for pleasure and he can use it to evolve. In case of an animal, only the body and a bit of mind are involved. In case of a common man, the body and the mind are totally involved but there is very little awareness. In case of an ascetic, all the three are equally participating - the body, the mind and the awareness. The animal and the common man are slaves of lust and it uses them as a vehicle; the ascetic gradually becomes the master of his lust and uses it as a vehicle instead. With the reversal of these roles, the whole relationship undergoes a change. What was more of a liability becomes more of an asset. In the hands of an ascetic everything becomes divine. Lust becomes love.

Lust in itself is neutral. It is our attachment to it and the resultant desires that convert a beauty into ugliness; a flower into a thorn; a blessing into a curse. From an aero plane, you can drop food and clothing for the flood struck homeless brothers, sisters, sons and daughters or you can drop an atom bomb on an assumed enemy; it all depends upon you. You can use your lust for creating poetry, music, relationships, meditation halls and homes or you can abuse it in a thousand different ways; your lust will never say, "What the hell are you doing with me?" It will allow your karma to unfold naturally just the way God allowed an atom bomb to be dropped on Hiroshima and Nagasaki. The wise man realizes his responsibility, uses everything and abuses nothing.

Lust is an energy and the river of every energy flows its usual course; the set pattern. When you entrench yourself in the space of witnessing and start looking at it from there, the set pattern has been disturbed. Now either the river can run over the banks or create a new course for its flow. In the case of someone whose meditation has not matured yet, it starts flowing over the banks. Without first constructing a canal system, he has built a dam in the path of the river. To be able to see your lust bloom into its purest possibility, you shall have to do a lot of work on the development of the witness because without it, you will have no base to stand on, no space to belong to. There is a whole range of techniques for developing the witness. You can choose the one that suits your soul.

Witnessing your lust will have two consequences; it will allow your lust to mature and it will lay down the foundation stone of a genuine renunciation where things have not been plucked prematurely but have been allowed to ripen and fall off by themselves. Renunciation is not about abandoning things; it is about things abandoning you. When the thieves of lust, anger, attachment, greed and ego see the watchman of witnessing, guarding the house of your soul, they go away disappointed. The watchman doesn't chase them; he just stays on guard. When all these different forms of energies are unable to play with your soul, they are left with no other option but to transform themselves into that which you will allow inside, which is - love. Once your soul has recognized love, everything else has to rearrange itself. Once you have tasted the real thing, you cannot be sold a fake. The pleasure of lust is fake; the real thing is love and it is beyond all pleasures and pains.

Lust is a great opportunity to go beyond the clutches of pleasure and pain. Ordinarily, we run away from pain and cling to pleasure. We do not realize that pleasure and pain are the two sides of the coin called life. If we cling to one, the other automatically falls into our lap. We can either take both or leave both. Distancing yourself from the pleasure of lust also means distancing yourself from the pains of life. If you can maintain this distance for a sufficient period, it can assist you in entering the dimension that doesn't belong to this world. It could turn out to be the greatest spiritual breakthrough of your life. Good and bad days will still come to you like the seasons of the year but they won't be able to throw you off your center. Like a firmly rooted tree that stays a witness to the four seasons of winter, spring, summer and autumn, you will remain untouched by the ups and downs of life. You will become stable and in harmony with the divine will.

Freeing yourself from the slavery of lust also means freeing yourself of the opposite sex. Life is very mysterious. As long as there is an ego and anger inside, there are thousands of enemies outside. When the ego is gone, there is no enemy. Similarly, when there is a lust inside, there are irresistible temptations everywhere; but when the lust is transformed; your love is not biological anymore. The root of our problems is always inside us and that root is our perception of reality. Our vision is clouded by our identity and we see the whole world through the glasses of our own clinging. As long as I have lust inside, I won't be able to see a woman the way God sees her. My seeing will get biased by my libido and the truth of her existence will get twisted while passing through my masculinity. A saint always sees a girl as a mother because that is her ideal possibility. All our media has used a woman as a sex object but that is her lowest form. Our markets are lust and desire oriented. You will find the picture of a sexy woman even on a packet of Tea because the seller knows what a common man desires deep within.

In the existence, there are plateaus of consciousness. The plant life is one plateau; the animal life is another and mankind is the next one. Then we have the plateau of the enlightened and the plateau of the Avatar. These plateaus have been proved by spiritual history and the experiences of all the ascetics. Now, the possibility of being able to witness our own lust should be considered as a major breakthrough. It is the simplest and most effective way of rising above the consciousness we are all trapped in. Without it, we are just a toy for our clinging to play with. Our clinging decides our life and we just go on living it like a fool. Take addiction to substances for example. Our clinging keeps on feeding on something that is harmful for us and we keep on suffering.

If your witness is strong enough, you will be able to perceive your lust in the form of a thick stem of vibrations that extends from the mind to the sexual organs. For its complete gratification as a hunger, it requires the body to fully participate in it, the mind to be fed with images of the opposite sex and thoughts created out of those imaginations to continuously pour into the emotion of lust created by it. The soul is also expected to join in by leaving the space of witnessing. When all join in the act, it takes its most natural form. But if the witness refuses to participate, the whole arrangement collapses. The mind is unable to sponsor the lust and the body also finds itself separated from the traditional mixture.

To make your witness, your sentry strong, you should feed it on love and compassion. Let lust take care of itself. Just worry about the health of your witness, your watchman. For the semi-enlightened, the best sources of compassion are kids, good friends of the same sex as you, plants, animals, mature old people, saints and nature. In the company of these, you will discover a dimension that is higher than lust on the scale of consciousness. Forget for a while that you are a man or a woman. Become one with a kid, become one with a plant, become one with a bird, become one with a lake, become one with the sky, become one with a tree, become one with water. You don't have to be a sexually charged male or female all the time. You don't have to offer your being at the feet of your lust. You can be much more divine than that, much more pure than that. Learn to forget about your sexual identity as much as you can and it will take you beyond polarities.

Preface Part II

     This part is a continuation of my work on the topic of spiritual liberation. It's the second part of this series. It is a package that I have tailored to assist you in understanding the major traps that are keeping us from realizing our true potential as a soul. I have used the words he, him, his etc. for the sake of simplification. They are not to be taken as discrimination between men and women. The soul does not have a gender, caste, race or nationality. It is beyond all these boundaries. Moreover, I have not written even a single alphabet with the intention of offending anyone but the nature of these topics is such, especially ego, that something could temporarily disturb you. Please take it like an Ayurvedic medicine that has got a bitter taste. I hope and wish that my efforts prove to be beneficial in the service of mankind and have some positive role to play in relieving the suffering that is there. May God bless us all. Namaste.

     Charanjit Singh

Part II

Ego, Attachment, Addiction, Fear & Greed

Chapter 4 - EGO

The wrestler thinks, "I am this strong body." The intellectual thinks, "I am this sharp intellect; this intelligent mind." The billionaire thinks, "I am these billions." The politician thinks, "I am the winner of the elections and this political power." The bureaucrat thinks, "I am this authority; this office." The supermodel thinks, "I am these good looks." The spiritualist thinks, "I am these spiritual powers." The family headman thinks, "I am the control I exercise over the family." The musician thinks, "I am this talent." The celebrity thinks, "I am this fame and these fans." We all start identifying with something other than the soul and this identification, this false self becomes our ego. Having an ego is like having two souls; the real consciousness and the virtual identification.

If there is a heated argument between a wrestler and an intellectual, the wrestler will try to point out the intellectual's physical weakness and the intellectual will point out the wrestler's average mind. We entrench ourselves in our identifications, fortify them, defend them and then attack the other from there. All disputes are disputes between identities. Two people who have come to realize their soul will never fight over anything. There are men and women who don't even exist in their body, what to say about the soul. You say something about their family and they become balls of fire. Their soul is a bundle of relationships that exist between them and their family members. These attachments are the bricks with which they have constructed their self. Any truth that has the potential to dissolve these bricks is perceived by them as a threat and therefore avoided, if not consciously then subconsciously. This soul of theirs has been tailored for them by their family members who have a vested interest in their spiritual handicap. In fact, they are all busy exploiting each other's emotional dependence. And it works through an unwritten mutual contract that says, "You feed my ego and I will feed yours; you protect my ego and I will protect yours."

The more egoistic someone is, the less he knows about his being. Ego is inversely proportional to the realization of your true being. The less light there is in the room, the more dark it is. And the more dark it is inside, greater are the chances of hitting against things and stumbling over objects. The more egoistic someone is, the more frequently he will bang into the divine laws that simply don't care who you are. Ego can attract towards itself nothing but suffering; suffering for the person who has cultivated it and suffering for everyone he comes in contact with. The Karma of an egoistic are such that they pull almost everyone down from their space of love, tolerance, compassion and forgiveness. The slumber of an egoistic is so deep that sometimes even death is unable to wake him up. People save their ego and choose to die. They choose to sacrifice their true self for a false identity.

Now if a wrestler is challenged by another into a bout, his ego has found the most ideal cause for its exhibition. But if he is told by a doctor that according to his medical examinations he is suffering from an incurable disease, his identity collapses like a house of cards. Our false self is nothing more than a house of cards. The slightest blow of destiny can bring it all down in a minute. Similarly, if a politician is campaigning for elections, it is the best situation his ego could hope for. But if one of his children is facing addiction problems owing to bad company and peer pressure, he is rendered helpless, disarmed and defenseless. Our false identity is incapable of standing the tests of truth; simply because it is false. You cannot walk on the surface of water even if it is as clear as glass and looks like glass.

The wrestler's ego is invested in the body, the intellectual's ego is invested in his mind and the spiritualist's ego is invested in his spirit. The one in a body is very solid, thick and tangible. It can be seen from a 100 yards. The one in the mind is a bit sophisticated and tough to catch. The one in the spirit is the most subtle and sophisticated one. It is called, "Suksham Ahankaar" in our books of wisdom. The wrestler wrestles with his body, the intellectual wrestles with his mind and the spiritualist wrestles with his spiritual powers; the Ridhis and Sidhis. An argument is nothing but a wrestling of minds and if you look closely into it you would be surprised to see that it is even more violent than the physical bouts. The cold war between two, so-called spiritualists, could be the most violent of all because here the intention is to harm the other on the deepest level of being. The wrestler could only break a leg, the intellectual could only break a self-esteem but a so-called spiritualist could break your heart, your very bloom; your essence.

Have you ever tried to study the ego of a disciplinarian? I have and this is what I have come to conclude. The disciplinarian entrenches himself inside a set of rules and regulations, an unwritten constitution and then expects everyone to follow it. These rules are his soul. The more rigidly he follows them himself, the more concrete his position becomes. But he doesn't feel concrete and lifeless; he feels strong. He is unable to sense the loss of fluidity and flexibility in his form. The rigidity in his presence makes people tight and tense, not blissful and at ease. The unwritten codes of conduct suffocate everyone and leave no space for the personality of the other. He is unable to see that what he really is, can exist outside these disciplines and exist without them, all of them and still be divine.

History has proved that often people choose to die than part away with their egos. Obviously, the pain of going beyond your ego must be more than the pain of death. And obviously they love their ego more than they love their life itself. Now, that is an extreme. The common man plays a clever trick. He keeps both his ego and his life. He never declares his ego very loudly and stays within the safe zones. The ascetic renounces both. So this is the whole range - the terrorist chooses his ego and parts away with his life, the common man parts away with nothing, keeps it all and the ascetic gives up all of it and clings to nothing. The terrorist thinks he has chosen death instead of life. But the truth is that he has chosen "Unconscious death instead of conscious death." Dying "To" your ego is dying consciously; dying "For" your ego is dying unconsciously. Dying consciously is like watching the funeral of your own identity - your false self, your virtual soul. It is painful because all the structures you had built out of ideologies and belief systems collapse and for a while you are unable to figure out what you are and who you are.

If a playback singer all of a sudden discovers that he is suffering from a throat cancer, it is not a tragedy - it is God's way of taking him beyond his false identity. If someone who is too much in the body becomes physically handicapped or ill, again it is God's way of introducing you to your true being. Destruction of the false self is essential because the true self and the virtual self cannot coexist. Light and darkness cannot coexist. One has to be sacrificed for the other. In fact, if you can offer your ego at the feet of God, you have made your greatest offering. God is not pleased by flowers and coconuts; God is pleased by the offering of your ego. Because though it is only an illusion with no substantial existence, it is a thick one and stands between you and your realization like a China Wall.

But what exactly is my ego made up of? It is what I think about myself, what I think about the existence and what I expect others to think about me. It is an image of myself that I have created in my mind. It has little to do with what I actually am; it has everything to do with what I think I am. The dictator never thinks he is a dictator. He thinks he is just a strict master; someone who brings about good with an iron hand. This image of a self-styled "Mr. Good" is his ego. The so-called spiritualist never thinks that he is someone who is harming and controlling others by abusing his mind and its powers; he thinks he is a God on a small scale. This image of a "Local God" is his ego. The head of a family who dominates and controls each and every other member of the family and has become a domestic Prime Minister never thinks he is suffocating the whole family with his invasion of their space; he thinks he is a compassionate caretaker. This image of a caretaker is his ego.

Ego is just an image. What significance do you think a mere mental image has in relation to the cosmos? How much invincible do you think is a cluster of beliefs? What are the chances of the survival of a soap bubble? It was there a moment ago - it's gone - "Gone in 60 seconds." Our ego is as fragile as a soap bubble and on some level of consciousness, we know that. That wisdom may not have surfaced and matured yet. But it is there. Hence all fear. No matter how much pride a bubble carries around, its vulnerability is too evident and obvious. The God's anchor in us is not afraid of anything, but the ego is. The ego is afraid of enemies because they have the potential to destroy it. Our immortality fears nothing and no one.

What do you think my ego would be? I think it would be the image of a talented devotional singer who knows about the existence quite a lot more than the average person and who has got the wisdom that can free people of their worldly entanglements. Even in my dreams, that image stays that way. Almost all my relationships revolve around that image. There are only a few where I am forced out of my identity; for example when my 8 months old baby gets his fingers caught up in my beard and he pulls out a hair or two in the act of balancing himself, at least for a moment, my image doesn't exist at all. The truth is that the relationships that exist outside the domain of my image are the most blissful. My ego becomes dormant and can rest for a while. I feel unburdened of a great baggage. But then, someone comes along and tells me that I made a lot of effort in the field of music but couldn't succeed accordingly and suddenly the whole anaconda of my identity wakes up out of nowhere. Ego is the most subtle and the most sophisticated of all spiritual puzzles.

When we are centered in this identity that we have created for ourselves, most of our actions are an effort to repair and construct our image. If we get a feedback from someone or somewhere that does not synchronize with our identity, we try in every possible way to restore our identity to its glory. For example, if a celebrity gets out of his car, shops around in a city famous for its awareness of the latest that is happening in the country and is not recognized by anyone, it could take him into an intense depression. His image has been shattered. His identity has failed the most practical test - the world. His pride has been injured. We really don't understand the core of the problem. The more desperately you try to save your ego, the more vulnerable you are. If you are investing in your ego, you are investing in a sinking Titanic. It is destined to sink; if not today then tomorrow. You should let it sink and save yourself. Even if it sinks, you can float. You can live even if it dies. You don't have to die with it; you don't have to sink with it.

The world knows you by your image. So if you care too much about this world, you will automatically have to care a lot about your image. You will find yourself looking into people's eyes all day and trying to find out what they think about you. You will have to dance to the tunes of this world like a puppet. Soon, you will be busy fitting into an identity that pleases this world but has nothing to do with your real self. In a very subtle way, you are reducing yourself from the creator's creation to the world's making. You will lose your touch with your godliness; your immortality. You will lose your touch with life itself because life will be reaching you after passing through the filter of your ego - your image. There will be no direct contact between you and the existence.

Do you think the flower blooms more and the moon shines brighter for the Prime Minister of a country than the clerk of a local bank or the rickshaw puller? No. Existence doesn't care for our tiny egos. With all the power that he has got, a dictator cannot dominate and control even a blade of grass; he can surely destroy it in the process of trying to do so. The existence does not care for any Aurangzeb, Duryodhan, Rawan or Hitler. These bubbles of ego are no big deal for the almighty. The egoistic tries to twist and turn the divine laws in order to suit his identity's need and therefore perishes. You cannot offer God at the feet of your ego; you can only offer your ego at the feet of God. The reality of this existence cannot be twisted to fit into an imagination of the mind. Every soap bubble thinks it is invincible but the one who is creating them knows the truth. He has witnessed so many of them come into existence, dance around a bit and then vanish. We are all bubbles of ego. We come into existence, exist for a while and then vanish. But there is a life beyond the ego.

When someone says, "This, this and this has happened to me and I am finished", he is saying the image of himself that he had created, is gone. If you say, "I am finished", you are standing inside your ego. But if you can say, "My ego is finished", you are standing in a space that is beyond the mind and beyond the ego. People who are too merged into their identity are unable to bear its demolish. They think, "That was all I was and it's gone; it's finished." They think of themselves as only that because they never tried to find what more there is to be. When the ego is shattered, you are forced into living without an identity for a while and this is where many of us give up. The mystery of life appears to have gone a bit too far. But if you can stay there for a while, the puzzle gets solved by itself and you discover that you are not only something other than what you thought you were, you are much more than that. From our perspective, the bubble has disappeared but from the perspective of the bubble, it has become one with the atmosphere. One way of being is lost but another way of being has been found. Nothing is finished - only an illusion has been eliminated.

Your ego is your sense of identity and an identity thrives on uniqueness and distinction. So anything that adds strength to these characteristics becomes food for the ego. Anything that differentiates between you and the rest nourishes the ego. Your name, your caste, your looks, your likes and dislikes, your attachments and possessions, your habits and addictions, your talents and your ambitions, even your past, pain and suffering, anything that belongs to you and defines you for the rest of the world becomes one of the veins that pump life into your ego. This is why people are so sensitive and touchy when it comes to their name, beliefs, religion and race. They derive their sense of self from all these things. When you touch any of these matters, you are touching the periphery of their "Self."

Have you ever wondered why people are so tired after a party, a get-together, a social occasion? They are tired because they have been spending a lot of energy on asserting their "Self." When so many egos come together, they start overlapping and intersecting. Boundaries start losing their definition, people start feeling as if they are just one more face in a gathering with nothing special to offer. They feel as if they are a crystal of sugar dissolving in a bucket of water. So they start asserting their peculiarity in civilized, intelligent and sophisticated ways. But the more sophisticated is your work, the more tiring it is. At the end of the day, you feel drained and fatigued and you just want to be alone for a while in order to recuperate from the, "Hangover of socializing."

The ego is not completely useless. Nothing useless was ever created by God. To evolve to a certain level of consciousness and to make certain achievements, the ego is required. It is an excellent vehicle. But thereafter, it must be discarded otherwise it becomes a "Stopping Stone." Life is like mountaineering; you can go up to a certain altitude in an air-conditioned car. Then there is certain distance you can travel on the back of a mule. But ultimately, you have to just "Climb." If your image of yourself is that of someone who is strong-willed and determined and who can accomplish almost anything once he has set his heart upon it, you are using your ego as a good vehicle. But if that image grows into someone who is respected by all, adored by all and worshipped by all, your ego has become a hindrance. Everything has to be kept where it belongs. You can add fried onion and garlic to a cooked vegetable but you cannot add them to a cup of tea or a milk shake. To use ego as a vehicle, you must be acutely aware of its strengths and its limitations. Our martyrs did that and produced great results.

Jumping out of your identity is almost like an outer body experience. Looking at an anger or a lust is easy; they are just an emotion. But ego is a very complicated thing. Witnessing your emotions is like looking at your hands or looking at your feet but witnessing the ego is like looking at the tip of your nose. It's tough. When you were witnessing your anger or lust you were a man of wisdom but that "Man of wisdom" is your identity, your image of yourself, your ego. So who will witness the ego? Who will witness that "Man of wisdom"? Only pure awareness can do that. This is what Shri Ram Dass is pointing towards when he is reciting the Mantra, "I am loving awareness." He is pointing towards 100% pure consciousness; the one that has no face; the one that has no name.

The ego doesn't like obscurity; it wishes to be noticed. It is continuously seeking attention and feedback. In obscurity, the ego starts fading. If people don't remember a celebrity anymore, he feels as if he doesn't even exist. His identity was his fan following; here go the fans - there goes the identity. The world created his identity, the world loved it for a while, cherished it for a while, then got fed up of it, started looking for something new and that's all. The ego seeks attention to assure itself that, "I am." Here is an observation you can make for yourself. Every time you have to stand in a queue for buying a ticket or paying a bill, you will notice that there is someone who finds it very difficult to be a point that goes into the making of a straight line. He either slides to the left or to the right to avoid the discipline of a queue. Why? Why can't he stand in a queue? - Because, the ego is very uncomfortable with being an invisible contributor. It wants to stand out and it wants to be, "The one and the only one." It wants to be noticed.

But no matter how much you invest in seeking attention and getting noticed, the actual "Is-ness" of ego can never grow beyond the shell of an egg. It is just an invisible hard membrane that contains all the stuff which goes into the making of your identity. Now, when the stuff inside an egg has matured into a small bird or animal, it's time for the shell to break. When your consciousness has matured to a certain degree, it's time for your ego to fall off. So, in a way, the ripening of your consciousness decides the fate of your ego. Therefore all techniques of meditation, all "Mantras", all "Sutras", all methods and secrets are just to assist your awareness in maturing and to dissolve the shell of your ego. If we break that shell prematurely, yolk pours out but if the shell falls off by itself, a living being steps out of it. What if the shell refuses to break? Well, the egg remains an egg. All the insanity in this world is because of this stubborn refusal; this hardening of the shells, this rigidity of the egos.

The ideal way to use your ego is to use it like a costume; you put it on when required and then you put it off. It's not required when you are looking at birds in the sky, it's not required when you are enjoying a meal, it's not required when you are playing with your kids and it's not required when you are listening to a good piece of music. You can live most of your life without bringing in your ego, without putting on that costume of your identity. The world knows you by your identity and therefore, in a subtle way, the world encourages your ego. You may have to put on that costume when you are dealing with the world, especially if your profession is a very image oriented one. But you can treat it as a costume, maintain your distance from it and then put it off and hang it in a closet. If you are wearing it all the time and treating it as if it were your flesh, you have missed the whole point. People who wear uniforms are often unable to take them off. Their identity gets too deeply embedded in their mind. A Brigadier behaves like a Brigadier even at 3 o clock in the morning and a police inspector behaves like a police inspector even at a cousin's wedding. Their costume has become their skin.

The presence of an egoistic always tends to pull you down into your identity and the presence of a Saint tends to pull you towards pure consciousness. An egoistic stimulates your ego just the way the opposite sex stimulates your lust. If you are not conscious enough, you will soon be responding to his provocations and fiercely defending your image. The greater is your investment in your image, the easier it is to provoke you into a confrontation. The egoistic is an "Irresistible Temptation" for your own ego. If you can stay conscious in the thickness of the moment when he or she is trying to damage your image by making repeated attacks on your identity, you can be liberated from your own attachment to it. If you can stand at a distance and be able to say, "Oh, he is just attacking what he thinks I am", you have stepped out of the eggshell. It won't be easy. We have been looking at life from inside that identity since thousands of years. All these incarnations, we have been thinking we are it and it is us. That belief has got its own inertia.

Why do you think an egoistic always avoids a Saint, feels jealous of him, hates him or even tries to harm him in one way or the other? Though we can ponder over that issue from many different angles but I will try to find an answer to this in a way that provides us with a bit more understanding of this thing called ego. The ego is threatened by the presence of those who do not consider images and identities of much significance. The rich man avoids a monk. The celebrity avoids a recluse. Our achievements constitute a great part of our identity and the presence of a Saint emphasizes on what we have not achieved yet. The poor man becomes poorer when he is standing next to a rich one; the sick person feels sicker at the sight of a healthy one. So, in the presence of a Saint, the egoist's spiritual poverty gets magnified and his "Virtual Self" is threatened. The pure consciousness of a Saint makes you feel as if you are no one, as if you are nothing. You feel that way because he is waking up that "No-one-ness" and that "No-thing-ness" in you. The devotee finds this peaceful; the egoistic finds this threatening. He finds it threatening because he loves his image more dearly than anything else. There is one more reason for the egoistic not being able to like the Saint. Ego feeds on duality and separation and the Saint emphasizes on oneness and brotherhood. When the ego does not get its regular diet, it feels starved and suffocated in the vicinity of an enlightened one. The egoistic would prefer the presence of another egoistic, even a rival or enemy to the presence of a Saint. The way our mind works is really strange.

The ego is also very uncomfortable with taking advice from someone or accepting someone as a teacher or Guru. Listening to someone's audio recording is easy but openly accepting someone as your coach, guide or mentor is very uneasy for the ego. It is so because the ego wants to feel adequate and self-sufficient. That sense of adequacy is destroyed when you have to openly admit that someone knows more than you and is in a position to coach you. Devotion, in a very silent and seductive way, takes a molecule of your ego from you every day. The devotee has to start his day by admitting his inadequacy and accepting his master as his mentor. He starts his day by making his ego uncomfortable and by offering a very small portion of it at the feet of his master. The more egoistic someone is, the more he or she will avoid seeking help in the moments of crisis. Ego does not want to take anything from anyone. It does not feel good being at the receiving end. Taking something from someone, then having to say, "Thank you" and being grateful for the assistance is alien to the ego. The ego always demands. "I have to have this", is the way ego asks for things. So that if you are unable to provide, it is you who feels inadequate. An egoistic beggar will beg in a way which makes you feel that if you don't give something, it is you who is poor, not the beggar.

The greatest prerequisite for being a great devotee is being comfortable with your inadequacy. Your love for your master has to be bigger than your ego for yourself. Your identity should be able to fit into the structure he has designed. If you are offering too much resistance to his methods, your identity is creating problems. While you see your ego as a sense of pride, self-esteem and confidence, the master sees it as a concrete shell that is not letting him inside. While your subconscious mind is busy designing ways of saving the ego, the master is busy creating a plan for the dissolving of it. This hide and seek between the compassion of the master and the desperation of your ego is one of the major aspects of the path of devotion - the "Bhakti."

What do you think, inside you, is hurt when you call up someone thrice and the person deliberately does not answer your call? It's the ego. By not answering your phone call, the person has questioned your significance and the purpose of your ego is to make you feel significant. It makes you feel you are something; you are somebody and you are not a burden on earth, a liability for God and a worthless consumer of life. All the achievement that has ever been made by man in any field, started from a thought, "I am significant", "I matter", or "I can make a difference in this world." But then, we start pouring all our energy into our significance and become too significant. Things go a bit too far. Our significance starts oozing out of every pore of our being and the blessing of ego turns into a curse.

Anyone who is living in a small apartment would like to own a bigger house, just because he is going to live in it. When we buy into the idea that our ego is what we are, we would like to own a bigger one. It is natural. We would like to become more significant. But the way each one of us architects that significance depends upon the kind of identity we have invested in. The Don of a mafia could get it by extorting billions from the richest celebrity in the country. A film maker or a music director could get it by winning the Grammy Award. A drug lord could get it by successfully smuggling a heavy amount of illegal stuff and an author could get it by writing a "Best Seller." The manner in which our ego works is really surprising and often very irrational. Like a parasite, it could kill the very organism it depends upon for its existence. Our ego can prolong our suffering so that it can survive, though it can exist only as long as we do. But why would a sickness have sympathy for the patient who suffers from it? It is for the patient to decide whether to keep it or discard it. Ego is an addiction to the sensation of significance and like any other addiction, you cannot afford to entertain it for too long.

Have you ever wondered why an egoistic tries to control everyone in his vicinity? He does so because control over others extends the radius of his identity and thickens his presence. He tries to become significant not by doing something of significance, but by making others insignificant. The control he exercises over others gives him a very strong feeling of "I am." He imposes his presence on others like an income tax. The presence of an enlightened being is also felt by everyone but it is never imposed on anyone. It is felt like the radiance of a full moon. After pulling others inside the circumference of his identity, the egoistic starts decorating his controlling tendencies by manipulating their needs, exploiting their shortcomings and abusing their dependence. His deepest motive is not to help you out; it is to keep you in a position where you need his help. If you are on your own, who will he control? The ego feeds on strange diets; it is nourished by invading, conquering and controlling. What could an Alexander possibly get from invading a kingdom, conquering it and adding it to his domain? That is pure ego. These inclinations are the essence of an ego - invading, conquering and controlling. Whether you use a sword or politics or spiritual power- it makes no difference.

There are basically only two ways of being - to be your body, mind and emotions or to be pure awareness, also called pure consciousness. If you identify yourself with the body, thoughts and emotions, you are an unrealized being and if you identify yourself with pure consciousness, you are an enlightened one. The whole dance of life is nothing but the different permutations and combinations that can be created out of these basic two ingredients. Between a Hitler and a Christ the whole world exists. Ego is a proof of your belonging to this world because when you have transcended it, you are, "In this world but not of this world." Ego proves that you have not yet become familiar with your immortality and that the distance between you and your mortal self has not yet crystallized. This body is certainly going to die. This mind, these emotions and this ego, they are all going to die. Why identify yourself with something that is going to die? Why cling on to something that is slipping away? Why try to freeze this river of life? Why not try to know that which was before we were born in this incarnation and which will be after it's over?

I had never realized this before but now I have noticed that when I start playing the harmonium, from the moment I press the first note, my identity as a musician starts taking its shape. My learning as a student, my struggle as an artist, my selections and rejections, my albums that were released but not promoted enough, my unfinished projects, my plans for the future, my dependence on professionals and my limitations and lacks - they all wake up from a slumber and join in the making up of my image - one by one. By the time I have played three compositions, the construction of this musician self of mine is complete and I feel like saying, "This is also me." Now, the point is, what do I do with this identity of mine that occupies more than 50% of the space of my "Virtual Self"? I can't throw it into a well because to survive in this world I would definitely have to put on one identity or the other. The world is not going to pay me for a being a good witness. So, what I think I can do is use this ego of mine to realize how our desires rob us of our divinity and how the temptations of this world keep us belonging to it.

I could be wrong but I think that when a person becomes a ghost after death and keeps on haunting the place he or she used to live in, it is most probably because the person had such a strong ego and such a big investment in the identification with his or her body and mind that even after death he or she has been unable to accept the truth of not existing in that form any more. Even death has failed to wake up the person out of the slumber of ignorance. The person has died in a state of spiritual sleep and is unable to accept the new dimension that surrounds the soul. It is as if you go to bed in India and when you wake up, you find yourself in Italy. And you are so attached to stuff in India that the only thing on your mind is - how to go back; legally or illegally. The more you invest in your ego, the less available you are to pure consciousness.

Laughing at your stupidities is a great technique for distancing yourself from your ego; your false self. The laugh creates a vacuum that serves as an invitation for pure awareness. When you laugh at yourself, you are the witness. The "At" that comes after the "Laugh" certifies it. An egoistic is unable to laugh at himself and even if he does so, he doesn't feel blissful after that; he feels as if he has stumbled over a block and unintentionally, done some damage to his identity. After some time you will find him repairing his image in some strange and sophisticated way. To laugh at yourself, you have to drop all that the ego uses to defend itself and become comfortable with the fact that you are a human being and not an Avatar. The one who cannot laugh at his falls cannot learn the real lesson contained in them. We distort the lesson when we identify ourselves with the one who made the mistakes. The ego twists and turns the wisdom contained therein. When you whole-heartedly laugh at yourself, at least for a few moments, you do not exist as an ego; you exist as a laugh.

Another way of pulling yourself out of that identification with your thoughts and that sense of "I" is by becoming highly alert in the presence of an egoistic, especially someone who can easily push your buttons. The Karma of an egoistic come from a very deep unconsciousness and if you start reacting to them, they can easily throw you off-center. But if you can stay alert in their presence, they can make you aware of your own ego more successfully than you could have done it alone. It is not fully formed when you are alone because a part of you is busy dissolving it. But when someone else attacks you, you can see your ego in its pure form. And that is your best opportunity to free yourself from it. It will be tough. You will feel as if someone is spitting on a life size portrait of yours right in front of you. But if you hold on to pure consciousness you will be able to say, "That's not me. It's my image, my identity which he or she is insulting." For the first time, you will realize that a lot of suffering in your life was because you did not know how to react to unconscious behavior and all that pain could have been avoided. Our reaction to the behavior of the unconscious is a reflection of our spirituality. The unconscious can make you all the more conscious if you decide not to react and just stay alert.

Now, what role do you think meditation has to play in freeing us of our identification with the mind? Meditation makes us aware of our ego's staple food - the internal dialogue; the incessant stream of thoughts. Stepping out of ego is the second part; the first part is being able to see it. How can you step out of a room that you can't even see? This is where most of the so-called spiritualists go wrong.

Without having recognized ego, they start assuming, even claiming that they have transcended it. How can you transcend something that you don't even know yet? Meditation creates in us the space and the vision required to watch our mind and all that it is capable of creating. Without the mind, an ego cannot exist. A mad man has no ego because he is unable to identify with the chaos in his head. When someone insults him, he shows no signs of an emotional injury, defense or retaliation. Meditation introduces us to the timeless dimension of pure consciousness from where you can look at all the things that exist in time or that need time to exist.

Anger can also be used as an opportunity to know your ego. Whenever anger shows up, try to find out where it is all coming from and you would be surprised to know that it is being sponsored by your ego. Whenever someone throws a stone into the pond of your ego, the ripples of anger are produced. Anger is the armor of the ego; its defense mechanism. With anger, ego saves and protects itself from all assaults. If you become alert in these moments, as alert as Austin Stevens is in the presence of a king cobra, the anger will gradually subside and your ego will be exposed to awareness. Your darkness will be exposed to your light. Even if your awareness is just a small lamp yet, it can dispel the darkness of a big hall. No matter how big your ego is, if left undefended and thus exposed to consciousness, it cannot stay for very long; though it will re-emerge when you are not firmly rooted in your consciousness and reassert itself. It's an old habit. It will die hard. Just stay on guard.

The ego is always busy repairing itself and rebuilding itself. Revenge is one of the ways in which the ego postpones its sublimation. The moment you decide to get even with someone who has injured your being in any possible way, you have offered your consciousness at the feet of your ego. But if you decide to forgive, you have decided to save the purity of your consciousness from the contamination of hatred. You will have to make that choice everyday and sometimes several times a day. As soon as you step into the world, you will encounter people whose actions are coming from a deep slumber. You will have only two choices, either to resist their ignorance and arrogance or to allow it as a part of the divine unfolding of life. You can either feed your ego and starve your consciousness or feed your consciousness and starve your ego. Both these choices will be always available to you.

Our sense of "I", our identity, is composed of several sub-identities. There is a parent in it, there is a professional in it, there's a husband or wife in it, there's a son or daughter in it, there's a brother or sister in it, there's someone who belongs to a certain religious sect, there's someone who follows a certain code of conduct as a citizen, there's someone who practices certain things for his or her physical, mental and spiritual health - it has got so many components that go into the structural build up of it like bricks and cement. We don't have to isolate these components in order to work on them. Once the whole identity is taken care of, the sub-identities will take care of themselves. We don't have to move the lamp of consciousness from one place to another; we just have to make the flame brighter and bigger so that no corner can escape its illumination.

Now, if everyone around you ignores you totally for a month, your ego will explode like a grenade - but why? Because you are unable to digest, the feeling of not existing, which others have created by totally neglecting you. That is exactly the reason why people who want fame can sometimes choose even negative publicity to make all heads turn towards them. When all eyes look at you, whether in surprise, adoration, awe or shock, your sense of "I" is restored. This is one of the most prominent causes of our domestic hells that break loose so frequently. When a child seeks attention, it starts crying; when an adult seeks attention he starts breaking things. Isn't it weird? - I mean the way our inside works. This complexity of our mind and emotions is what goes into the making of this insane world. And the greatest challenge for man today is - how to stay sane; how to live in this asylum without going mad.

When events happen around us without any kind of our participation in them, we feel left out. If this continues, it can make us feel powerless and helpless. Now, the sense of powerlessness is the polar opposite of the sense of "I". It is very difficult for the two to coexist. Ego wants to feel in control of things and feel powerful. This is the core cause of all the power trips, power struggle, hunger for power and even battling for it. An egoistic wants nothing around him to happen without his prior consent. This consent strengthens his sense of "I", makes it thick and tangible. It leaves no doubt in his mind about "I am"; about "Him being". The stamp that someone applies on a document to make it valid becomes that person's ego. That stamp is nothing but the prior consent that I just mentioned. But if you are conscious, this feeling of being left out, being neglected and ignored can be used to know that element which feels all of this. It's your ego. You wanted to know what it is. Well, this is it. So, don't get attention by exploding; just watch your ego and break those old patterns that have been living through you all these decades.

There are basically only two ways of looking at life; you can look at it from within your ego or you can look at it from your consciousness. Life is neutral as such, but when it passes through the prism of our thoughts and our sense of "I", it changes. It gets dyed in the color of our thinking. Ego survives by labeling, analyzing and criticizing everything. These things sharpen its edges and define its outlines. It stands out from the rest of the existence with all this. But life gets distorted by all this. The purity of the existence is lost in passing through the mind. Absolute existence can only be seen with pure consciousness. Then you don't even call a tree a tree and a sky a sky; you just look at them and let their magnificence be absorbed by your being. What Shri Ram Dass often refers to as, "The dance of life" can be experienced only by the consciousness; the mind is incapable of understanding the dance. So don't label, don't judge, don't analyze and don't criticize and your ego will soon be out of business. Try to look at this existence with the curiosity of a new born baby and secrets shall be revealed to you.

Every time our ego is shattered, it tries to put the broken pieces together, repair itself and rebuild itself. If you just want to survive, then this rehabilitation of the ego is a great assistance. But if you wish to be liberated, you have to hinder this process since the rebuilding of our ego is only an invitation to another crisis. So, instead of putting the broken pieces together, just keep on watching those pieces and gradually you will start realizing that what has been shattered is nothing but an illusion. Whatever you thought you had lost was only lost in a dream and the existence is welcoming you to a fresh morning that has nothing to do with your nightmares. The existence has nothing to do with our sense of self. When I look at a bird, the bird doesn't think, "Oh! Charanjit Singh is looking at me." The existence just doesn't care who I am and what I think about myself. My ego is my own brainchild; my own creation. And if I really wish to know the existence as it is, I have to drop this filter through which I am looking at it and allow the actuality of life to come in direct contact with my being, my consciousness. Let life meet life and there be no mind to spoil the moment.

The most prominent feeling that accompanies our sense of self like a shadow is the feeling of incompleteness. There is this urge to add something to itself and become more than what it is. The ego never feels whole or 100% and the reason for this is that it has cut itself off from the existence and a part that has been cut off from its source can never feel whole. Someone is busy adding possessions to his ego, someone is busy adding triumphs of all kinds to it, someone is busy adding knowledge to it, someone is busy adding spiritual powers to it and it still keeps on asking for more. We never give it a thought. We never stop for a moment and try to find out what is it inside us that is never satisfied, that never feels complete. We look at the world and think "It's Okay" but it isn't. Something is wrong and there is something that we need to step out of in order to look back at it. Once you are out of it, you will find that the whole mankind is trapped in ego and all the pain, suffering, hatred and violence is because of this trapping; this basic displacement of the sense of self. Someone once asked a saint about the secret for enlightenment. "Nothing much", he said, "You uproot it from here and plant it there." Now, he was a farmer and was working in his fields with saplings. So he used his own terminology to explain the shift of consciousness from the virtual self to the real self.

Chapter 5 - ATTACHMENT

When someone passes away, the emotional thickness and heaviness that is there in the immediate vicinity of such a happening is chiefly because of attachment. It is so thick; almost like an emotional cloud that cuts off a family from the luminosity of life. There is guilt in it, there's self pity in it, there's the pain of separation in it, there's the sense of loss in it; it's one of the greatest emotional challenges that come with this human incarnation. But can we eradicate it from our incarnation? No. Our death is decided even before our birth. Our purpose of visit and our duration of stay on this planet are determined even before we show up. We all come here with a return ticket.

The flux of life includes death and departure for its maintenance and attachment is our trying to hold on to whatever we have got. We don't want life to flow like a wild river; we want it to be still like a swimming pool. We are not comfortable with too much of change in our world and therefore try to include as much of permanence as we can, in the designing of our world. It compensates for the change that is an intrinsic characteristic of life and which we can do nothing about. We don't build great houses and buy great cars just for physical comfort; they bring some permanence to our life. The absence of life in these things is a protection against mortality. We do not wish to construct too much of our world with things that contain life because whatever contains life is bound to change.

Parents bring up their children, but then, are unable to stop and keep on bringing them up. All the problems that a man or a woman faces with his or her in-laws are basically because of attachment. The attachment of one becomes interference for another. The parents try to freeze the love that existed between them and their children and refuse to accept the changed form of it in which they will have to share it with someone. Since love is so rare these days, it is the one thing that people most fiercely cling to. But they do not realize that their very clinging converts that love into something else. A nectar becomes a poison. The parents cling to a child because that was all they had got. They found love in that child and they started assuming that it is the only place where they can find it. Decades flow down the river of life but they think it is the same that they bathed in.

A great portion of our sense of self, our ego, is invested in objects outside us. Attachment is the chord that connects our ego with images of these objects – living as well as non living. If you take away all the ego from this, what's left behind is love; the chords are even stronger but they are qualitatively different. The chords of attachment are invisible but stronger than steel. A part of our ego is invested in our car, a part of it is invested in our house, a part of it is invested in our children and a part of it is invested in our spouse. A threat to any of these means a threat to our existence. A harm to any of these implies a harm to us and a loss or a fear of loss of any of these implies a loss of our, "Self." We do not totally exist in ourselves; we exist in others. We are scattered all over our world and this world is held together by strings of attachment. If anything in our world moves away from us, our attachment grows in magnitude and resists the movement. So we have our ego in the centre, objects all around and each of them is connected to it with an elastic band of attachment that cannot be seen. In the Indian sacred books, it is known as "Moh."

In all the spiritual traditions, there has been a great emphasis on giving and renunciation (Daan and Tyag). There is an absolute logic in that. With each and every act of giving, a thin thread of attachment falls off. From threads, you can then graduate to strings and deal with the thicker stuff of your virtual self. When you consciously give away something or you give away an addiction, you drop away a thread of attachment by choice but if something is taken away from you without your prior consent, it is like snapping off a thread or string. Snapping is painful because your whole being was not prepared for it. Deaths and departures are therefore very painful. A string of attachment has been pulled beyond its elasticity and snapped off against your will. It is like plucking off an unripe fruit from a tree. It is premature for the soul and shocking for the ego. A Guru always prepares you in advance for all that is inevitable and which he sees approaching you according to your own evolution or Karma.

When there is no giving in your life and all your acts are centered on taking and accumulating, you are basically strengthening your strings of attachment. The more attached you are to things, the more resistant you will be, to the flow of life and evolution of souls. You would expect everything to stay the way it is and to stay where you have put it while designing the world that suits your ego. You would even try to cut your objects of attachment from the rest of the world as a precautionary measure against influence and change. If someone is dependent upon you for anything, your attachment will force you into exploiting that dependence and trying to keep it the way it is so that the connecting link between you and the person doesn't fade away.

The strings of attachment are like the gravitational pull. Every time an object moves away from you, your attachment pulls it back and the force with which you pull is inversely proportional to the distance between you and the object you are attached to. When someone you love goes away for a week or two you start missing the person. The strings of attachment thicken and start dominating your being. The absence of one person becomes greater than the presence of all the rest. But this happens in love also. Even Avatars miss the ones they love. So there is nothing wrong with missing someone.

The problem is, "Who is missing someone? Is he residing in ego or awareness?" If you are centered in ego, all your relationships will be an attachment; if you are centered in pure consciousness, all of them will be love. Attachment is nothing but love that has been contaminated by your false sense of self.

When you are attached to someone, it is because that person satisfies one of your emotional needs. Instead of looking for a source within you, you assume that if you want this thing, you can only get it from that particular relationship. Now you will become selfish, possessive and jealous. Your ignorance will have no concern for the wellbeing of the other. You will extend the darkness of your ego in all directions and try to cut off all your relationships from the infinity of the existence. Ego knows nothing about the good of all and has nothing to do with it; it only knows about its own sense of lack and insufficiency, its desires and demands, its prides and prejudices, its false beliefs and its auto suggestions, its continuous struggle for survival. The world of an egoistic is like the darkness inside a vessel that has been put upside down in a room illuminated with bright, white light. The attachment of one can jeopardize all the relationships of the other with its insecurities.

Lets' suppose you fall in love with the chirping of a bird sitting on the branch of a tree. And now you want to have a regular supply of that chirping. So you somehow manage to catch that bird and put it inside a cage. You feed it with dry fruit and chocolates and time your feeding in such a way that the bird has to chirp for it. Do you think it's the same bird and the same chirping that you fell in love with? This is what we do to relationships with our ego and our attachment. We kill the whole thing. But in love, the other's well-being becomes primary for you. Instead of buying cages, you will plant trees so that birds come, chirp and fly away. You will not exploit them into chirping; you will silently wait for them to do so out of their own happiness. Love plants trees while attachment buys cages.

Three of our greatest attachments are identity, possessions and relationships. If we can detach ourselves from our identity, our ego, the other two automatically fall off because possessions and relationships are nothing but external objects in which our ego has been invested. It is as if each one of us is an invisible solar system in which all our attachments revolve around our ego. When we shift our residence from the ego to pure awareness, our whole world undergoes a change. The rigidity and resistance of ego is replaced by an acceptance of the flux of life. The meaning of possessions and relationships changes and the wisdom of impermanence becomes an integral part of your knowing.

Too much of attachment also points towards the fact that the truth surrounding death has not yet been digested and assimilated by your being. You can't understand death by standing unconsciously at the funerals of others; you understand it only by becoming aware of your own guest appearance on this planet. This one truth can destroy most of your illusions and when you include it in your life you cannot live the way you used to. You cannot sleep like a log with this naked sword hanging over you from the rooftop. You cannot go on hoarding your life with things when you have fully realized that you are going to leave this plane of reality with nothing but a soul. This is exactly why you will never ever find more than enough around a real Saint. Every time he realizes he has got something more than enough, he gives away that "More" so that he is left with just "Enough." So even if an enlightened being has got a private aero-plane, it must be his necessity. His time must be that precious and his responsibility must be that big. But if you take the plane away and give him a bicycle instead, he would be at total ease with that also. That's renunciation.

It is very important for us to understand the difference between enjoying all that life has to offer and getting attached to it. You can have 10 rupees and be attached to them and you can have billions and not be attached to them. History has witnessed many enlightened kings. The problem is not with the stuff outside; the problem is with the clinging of our mind and the solution is in stepping out of the mind. The mind is cut off from abundance. It is poor. Obviously it will cling to whatever it has got. But our awareness is rich. Our mind is a demanding beggar; our awareness is a generous king. Just stop identifying yourself with the beggar and start identifying with the king. Step out of your mind and step into awareness. Like landing on moon, it can be a small step for man but a great leap for mankind. It can lay down the foundation for the next world or it can save a bit of this for the future.

With the inclusion of the truth surrounding death in your realization, your consciousness can see the thread that runs through the beads of your incarnations. You can see the continuity hidden behind the interruptions, the immortality behind these births and deaths; this dying, getting reincarnated and dying again. You can see that the world has been taken away from you and then given back to you thousands and thousands of times. So, you can live in it and enjoy the temptations for as long as you wish to. You can see that all the loose ends are tied again and you pick it up from where you had left. All your unfulfilled desires, all your dreams that did not come true, all your relationships that did not work out - it's all handled for you and in a much more efficient way than you could have done it yourself. The master of all relationships – the relationship between you and this existence does not come to a dead end with your death. It unfolds again; with the fragrance of your uniqueness emanating from it. When this wisdom becomes a part of your awareness, you no longer feel the urge to get inside your identity and try to remain in control of everything. A "Letting-Go" feels more sensible and natural to you than clinging to everything and fiercely struggling to maintain your control over things that are beyond your control.

Now, we are attached the most to things that provide us with a sense of security. It could be physical security, it could be emotional security or it could be even spiritual security. These things are our protection against the harsh ways of this world. Our house provides us with physical security, our business provides us with financial security, our relationships provide us with an emotional security and our religion provides us with a spiritual security. We seek security. Maybe, this need for security has evolved through the centuries, from that man in the cave who protected himself and his family from wild animals and natural disasters. Instead of wild animals, we have wild human beings and instead of natural disasters, we have relationship problems. So we seek protection in the refuge of our attachments. But we forget to take one factor into account - change. Houses are washed away in floods right in front of the owner's eyes, businesses can collapse, relationships can fall apart and the fragile thread of religious faith can be snapped easily by blows of fate. Change is God's protection against decay and it is through change that life is regenerated. The best way to strike a balance between our deepest need and God's way is to embrace all change and take refuge in that which is constant - "Pure Consciousness."

I have brought up two babies and I know that if there is something in their hand and you need it, you have to give them something else to play with. The same holds true for us also. Our hold on the material is loosened only and only when we have got enough of the spiritual. The renunciation of all the worldly pleasures by the enlightened beings certifies one thing - that the bliss of enlightenment is greater than all the pleasures of the world put together. But you renounce things when you get enlightened; you don't get enlightened by renouncing things. This distinction must be understood. Our attachments only indicate that we are still trapped in the mind and the ego and the dimension of pure consciousness has not yet bloomed in us. So we need not worry about our clinging; rather we ought to become more aware, more conscious and let our consciousness take care of our clinging.

When you love, the well-being of the other is primary; your comfort is secondary. When you are attached, your comfort is primary and the other's well being is secondary and sometimes not even secondary. When your child grows up into an adult and gets married, if you love your child you will assist him or her in coping with the challenges of a married life. But if you are attached, you will keep on interfering in his or her life and rather than solving your kid's problems you will be a problem itself. Many of the marriages are ruined by external interference, especially the interference of attached parents. Attachment makes you blind to the obvious and you start twisting and turning all truths to make them fit into a reality that suits your ignorance, your ego. You go on ruining things and you go on justifying yourself. You are unable to accept the change in your relationship with your child which accompanies his or her marriage. Love embraces change and finds new ways of giving and new ways of relating. Think about God. It feeds clothes and shelters even those who don't believe in it - that's love.

A woman carries an infant inside her womb for nine months. What if she gets attached to this unborn baby and refuses to give birth to it for the fear of having to share the baby with the world? The baby will die. Our relationships also go through a lot of psychological wombs. Too much of attachment can kill them. We have to accept the divine flow of events and create space in us for the growth of our relationships. After a child comes out of the mother's womb, it plays around for 3-4 years. But this childhood is yet another womb. Now, it's time to send the kid to school. And the school is also a womb. After passing out of the school, the boy or girl has to go to college and graduate. After graduation, is a job, then a married life and then bringing up children, a shift of generation and so on. It never ends. We never stop growing. Anyone who resists this change is bound to break and suffer. It is too powerful to be resisted. But if you start flowing with it, the power of the current becomes yours.

Now, what could be the purpose behind the creation of this element of attachment by God? You will find the answer if you observe carefully the life of birds and wild animals. If there were no attachment at all, who would take care of the newborns? Without it, the survival of a species would be almost impossible. Imagine a wild buffalo giving birth to a calf and then just walking away as soon as it is born, leaving it at the mercy of lions, wolves and hyenas. It is attachment that makes it guard, protect and feed this vulnerable creature that has just opened its eyes in a strange and unknown world. It is attachment that builds a nest and if you examine a nest and think about the stuff that it is made up of, you would get an idea of the mind and the emotion that has gone into the making of it. Attachment was created by God to construct, not destroy; to bring up kids, not possess them; to build relationships, not ruin them and to help each other, not torture each other. We basically lack the skill that is required to deal with the elements of life.

One side of the coin of attachment is emotional comfort and the other side is suffering. The amount of suffering at the loss of something or someone you are attached to, is directly proportional to your attachment to the object. So if you don't want too much of suffering, don't get too much attached. But how will you do that? Will you check your attachment with an instrument and try to find out how much it is? Will you run away from relationships and intimacy for the fear of getting attached to all this? Will you stop coming close to people for the fear of their moving away from you? Will you shut your doors to abundance for the fear of being forced by circumstances to live in lack at some stage of your life? Will you stop using material comforts for the fear of losing your soul to the temptations of this world? – It does not work that way. You have to live in the thickness of the world, the "Sansaar" and still be untouched by it.

The secret lies in understanding that it is the mind that clings, not that which is capable of looking at the clinging of the mind. But we don't have enough of it - the awareness. Therefore, the mind dominates our being. Clinging is the nature of the mind. When you give something to a six months old baby, it plays with it for a while and then takes it towards its mouth and tries to eat it. No matter what you hand over to the baby, it behaves the same way. That is the nature of a baby. Similarly, the nature of the mind is to cling. You give anything to the mind; it starts clinging to it. If you give it materials, it will start clinging to materialism. If you give it knowledge, it will start clinging to knowing. If you give it spirituality, it will start clinging to spiritualism. You can't expect anything else from the mind. It was made to cling. So let it cling. Let it be the way it is and look for a refuge outside the mind. The problem of attachment cannot be solved from within the mind.

An ordinary man resides in the mind and occasionally steps out into the space of pure consciousness. He is unable to stay there because he does not identify himself with it. He identifies himself with his mind. So he just touches that space for a moment or a few moments at the most and then jumps back into his mind - his residence. The awakened one resides in pure consciousness and jumps into the mind whenever required, only to go back to his home. So they are rooted in different dimensions. Attachment is an indication of being rooted in the mind and its remedy is in all those techniques that assist you in cultivating awareness. Because before you start living in it, you have to have a home to live in. Awareness is going to be your new home and meditation is all the techniques that help you in building that home; in constructing that home. Whether it is simple mindful breathing, which is the enlightened monk Thich Nhat Hanh's favorite or dynamic meditation designed by Acharya Rajneesh, the purpose is simply to build up your awareness. From a fleeting dimension that strikes across your being like a lightening in the sky, awareness has to be built up into something you are as comfortable with as the room you are sitting in right now. An acquaintance has to be developed into a familiarity.

The nature of awareness is the taste of reality. As you become more aware of the ways of God, your own perceptions start falling off like dead leaves falling off in autumn to create space for fresh ones. Awakening is the spring season of your soul - the "Basant Ritu" as we call it in India. When you become aware, you realize that the existence does not care for our own ideologies, philosophies and assumptions. Truth is not affected by our personality. Our personality is our own baggage and to be carried around by us, not by that which is beyond all these localized clouds of guess work. Attachment is one of those things that automatically get corrected when our wisdom is attuned to the "Isness" of life. The pain of death and departure or the pain of separation is still there but now it is not cut off from reality because of lack of knowing and is not caught up in the four walls of ego. It is in harmony with that which holds this world together. The other side of the coin gets added to it - "The wisdom of impermanence".

When we get attached to our body, we forget that it is going to age and die. When we get attached to our identity, we forget that it is only our virtual self, not our true self. When we get attached to our possessions, we forget that they are just things to be used and then passed on to someone else or thrown away. When we get attached to our relationships, we forget that each and every one of us has got his or her own Karma to unfold and a relationship with the existence which is beyond our control. We forget. We forget and therefore we suffer. The job of awareness is to remind us. The more aware we become, the less we tend to forget and the ones who become fully conscious cannot forget even if they want to. So, they don't have to remember any more.

As I mentioned earlier also, giving has got a great deal of hidden potential in loosening and thinning our strings of attachment. But that potential can be accessed only if an act of giving is done with the emphasis on the other and done as consciously as possible. With the emphasis on the other, your awareness has to expand in order to include the other and when it is done consciously, it has got a greater probability of becoming a part of your awareness rather than your ego. People give, but when their attitude is, "Look at me; I am giving", it loses its purity. Sometimes we give just to get rid of the receiver. If I am having a meal and a crow starts disturbing me by hopping around and by making these sharp sounds, I would obviously throw a chunk of bread to keep it occupied while I enjoy my meal. We give to the beggars also just to get rid of them. This kind of giving is not the one I am talking about. The act has to be pure and it has to come out of compassion.

An act of giving is pure when your joy comes from thinking about some need of the other being satisfied, when you are able to feel the joy of the other and include it in your being. Such an act can pull you out of your separation and duality, for a few moments at least and introduce you to the taste of the oneness behind all the separations and dualities. If the strings of oneness are strengthened and thickened, the strings of attachment are automatically weakened and thinned. A pure act of giving reveals to you the wisdom of "Give and you shall receive" and you come to really know that there is something else going on behind the obvious; something which is smaller than the electron and bigger than the milky way. Gradually you start realizing that your attachment is not a protection from insecurity but a handicap that makes you even more vulnerable by cutting you off from the infinity and vastness of the silent mystery surrounding you.

So, the first thing is, give with the emphasis on the other and the second is, give consciously. In our holy books, an act of giving, if followed by the ego claiming it, is described as the bath of an elephant. We get dirty and then wash ourselves by bathing in water while an elephant first bathes in water and then pours mud over its body. When ego comes in and ruins everything, the chance of giving to dissolve your separation and duality is lost. You have to stay alert and see if your charity is contributing to the growth of your compassion or the growth of your ego. There are many whose donations are just another investment of their ego and whose acts of charity come from "I donate also" kind of attitude. There is no purity in it. It must be pure for it to be of any significance.

The strings of attachment are very powerful; very thick. Imagine the thing that connects someone, who has been sentenced to life imprisonment, to his family. Imagine the emotional bonding between a soldier and his family; a soldier who is fighting insurgents on a strange land far away from home. Imagine that which exists between a family and a family member who is going to die or the vacuum created by the passing away of someone's loved one. Imagine the density of the helplessness of someone who has lost every bit of his possessions in a riot or a natural disaster or someone who is going through a divorce which he or she never wanted. Imagine someone who has come to know that he or she is suffering from an illness that has been declared incurable by the general physicians. It is all so dense; so thick. The bonds of attachment are so strong that they can connect you to someone who has died and got reincarnated if you have been missing him or her very deeply, though you won't be able to recognize your dear one because of the new body and identity he or she has gotten into.

If we don't bring awareness into the situation, there is no end to the suffering that our attachment can create for us. It is awareness that enables us to see the other side of the coin which has got suffering on one side. It was always there. Truth is always there. But we cannot see it with the mind alone. If it were possible to realize the ultimate truth with the mind alone, all the great scientists should have got enlightened. But they didn't. They didn't because they could not identify themselves with that which is neither the body nor the mind or the breath or the emotions. That which can stand at a distance from all these and witness them, is the one that can rescue us from all our traps. And attachment is definitely one of the most powerful traps.

It is awareness that creates in us, the space required to accommodate the change and impermanence which is an essential part of life. Without standing at a distance from the things that we are most attached to i.e. our body, our identity, our possessions and our relationships, we cannot get a glimpse of the bigger picture or the dance of life. But where would you stand to watch all this? Awareness is that dimension from where you can watch the true face of reality. The absence of an understanding of the true nature of reality is the major cause of our attachments. We get caught up in the fear and insecurity of our comfort zone and are unable to open the gates of our being to the river of life that flows through us. To flow with that river, you have to embrace change and impermanence. There is no point in the banks of a river getting attached to the water that flows through them. The banks should just watch the flow and enjoy the company of that which is not flowing from here to there i.e. the essence of a river or the "Riverness" of it.

Too much of attachment also implies that you have not yet had enough of the world, the "Sansaar" and that you still have some great expectations from it. The ones who have had enough of it are very acutely aware of all the temptations that try to seduce the mind into wanting and desiring. They don't jump into buying things and they don't jump into relationships. They have come to know that the joy derived from the fulfillment of desires and the consumption of things is like a sand dune - now it is; now it is not. Just now it was there and now there's not even a trace of it. When you discover that the joy you have been looking for is within you, all which is outside you automatically becomes secondary. You may love it even more than you did before but you won't try very hard to squeeze happiness out of it. If something works, you will stay with it; if something doesn't, you will move within. The cultivation of awareness within you is like the backup battery of an electrical appliance which keeps it going during a power cut. Attachment means your joy is totally dependent upon your body, identity, possessions and relationships. And when you are dependent upon something, you cling to it like a baby clings to a mother.

Awareness pulls your soul out of the world; out of the "Sansaar." The energy which was being sucked by the hungers and gratifications of this world starts moving into a dimension where there is no hunger. Since there is no hunger, there is no chase to satisfy it either; hence the peace, the rest and the joy. And when you have got enough of it within you, your relationship with this world is not that of taking from it or squeezing it for something or the other; your relationship is that of sharing with the world whatever you have got. The selfish strings of attachment are replaced by bonds of compassion and the stagnancy of the mind is replaced by the flow of pure consciousness.

Attachment not only keeps you stuck in the world, it also makes you incapable of understanding the role of suffering in the bigger scheme of things. When you are too attached to your body and your ego, you are unable to understand your own suffering and when you are too attached to your loved ones, you are unable to understand their suffering. And according to the wisdom of the enlightened master Thich Nhat Hanh, without an understanding of suffering, there can be no compassion and there can be no forgiveness. He goes on to say that the willingness to forgive is not enough; you have to have an insight into your own suffering and the sufferings of those who make you suffer, in order to forgive them. Attachment diverts all your energy in the direction of trying to get rid of suffering as soon as possible instead of allowing it to be there and getting to know its divine purpose and its real value. When we get too busy in the relieving of suffering, we are deprived of the understanding of it. The most important thing about suffering is to know why it is there in the first place. Half of it is relieved, just in the knowing of this. But because of our attachment, we identify with the suffering and because of this identification with it, it gets exaggerated.

A good practice to keep your attachment in check is to make a list of the fifteen things you are most attached to and then live without them for two weeks. It would be a kind of fast for your attachment. Maybe you have been over-eating your possessions, identity and relationships and need some break from all of them for a while. You can design this retreat in your own special way and choose a place where you won't be disturbed. You may come across some strong winds of fear, anger and the feeling of being unloved but if you allow them to be, as long as they are and stay rooted in your consciousness, they will soon pass away and leave you alone with a peace that you may have never known before - the taste of detachment. Acharya Rajneesh calls it, "Vairagya Ka Anand." You will feel like having been introduced to your absolute self - the one that is going to stay with you even after your incarnation is over. You will also discover how you have been leaning on others for love and spiritually handicapping yourself. The insights gained from such a practice will take away a lot of the clinging from your relationships and make them more spacious and fluid.

It is very essential for you to realize that consciously stepping out of the clinging of the mind is a very great spiritual effort. It is not something you can accomplish when you run out of all the energy that you have got. Just as we require a lot of physical vigor to go on with a heavy workout in a gymnasium, spiritual practices also demand a great deal of spiritual vigor. The tendency of the mind is to postpone things. The world, the "Sansaar" is not that easy to renounce; the temptations are not that easy to resist. The decision to stay conscious is not that easy to make when you have got so many intoxicating alcohols all around you; the alcohol of sex, the alcohol of power and ego, the alcohol of wealth and fame and the alcohol of anger and violence. Saying "No" to all of them requires a lot of sincerity and strength. No one becomes a Buddha with half hearted attempts. You have to be very honest with yourself and totally committed to truth. Most of us fail to see the suffering which Siddhartha went through in order to bloom in the form of Gautama the Buddha. We see the lotus but we fail to see the mud; the mud of suffering - chosen as well as un-chosen.

Chapter 6 - ADDICTION

Part 1

A Quick Look At Addiction

Before we talk about an addiction, let us see what some of the greatest thinkers have to say about a habit.

1) "The chains of habit are too weak to be felt until they are too strong to be broken."

Samuel Johnson

2)"Everything you are used to, once done long enough, starts to seem natural, even though it might not be."

Julian Smith

3) "First you make your habits; then your habits make you."

Lucas Remmerswaal

4) "Habits are only useful if they are broken as soon as they cease to be advantageous."

Somersat Maugham

5) "We become what we repeatedly do."

Sean Covey

6) "Your net worth to the world is usually determined by what remains after your bad habits are subtracted from your good ones."

Benjamin Franklin

7) "Habits are habits, not to be flung out of the window by any man but to be coaxed down the stairs one step at a time."

Anonymous

If I were to define an addiction, I would define it as a habit that is not good for your well being; that you want to quit, but are unable to. It could be anything. It could be sugar, caffeine, alcohol, cocaine, violence, unholy relationships, money, selfishness, egoistic conquering, using foul language, lethargy, miserliness, domination, manipulation, jealousy, anger, lust or anything that brings you down as far as your overall wellbeing is concerned. We are all addicted to something that has a negative value for our self development. You may be drinking more anger, jealousy, or lust on a daily basis than an alcoholic drinks alcohol, without being aware of it. So, the first thing we all ought to do is take a fresh and objective look at our weaknesses and stop camouflaging them or gold plating them.

The second thing is to become fully aware of the negative potential of an addiction. We should neither under estimate it nor overestimate it. Just look around and see what harm have bad habits done to people's lives. There is no need to personally go through all the disasters on earth to become wise and experienced. You can learn from the mistakes of others who are just as human as you are. I have witnessed addictions ruining families and converting heavens into hells with their vicious cycles. It was the pain of those tragedies that forced me to go into the depth of this social evil and try to save as many as I can from the clutches of a catastrophe. My intention is to try to remove all such thorns from your soul that are a continuous pain for you and your loved ones. From my own experience, I know how painful they are.

Addictions can cause physical, mental and spiritual corrosion. They keep on nibbling at your body, mind and soul. The body becomes weak, the mind imbalanced and the soul out of tune.

They can throw your whole life into a comma and halt your progress on all levels. The control that an addiction has upon you can do a lot of damage to your self esteem and thus distance you from your own godliness. An addiction can teach you to lose in the game of life itself. Every time you give in to your habit, you are subconsciously learning to lose and to give in. You are learning defeat. In a mysterious way, an addiction can affect each and every aspect of your life. There is nothing that remains untouched. An addiction throws you off the track of purpose and sends your life in a different direction. We all know that when the direction changes by even a few degrees of an angle, the destination can change by thousands of kilometers. If it goes unchecked for too long, a bad habit can make your life land somewhere you had not even dreamt of. My purpose is not to scare you by telling you what could happen to you, but to save you from painful possibilities. The wisdom of a sensible man lies in anticipating the future and then initiating some changes to make it as beautiful as he can. If we don't anticipate, it can happen in actual. Your job is to use your fear to your advantage.

Addictions can also become an obstacle to your spiritual evolution. Dr. Wayne Dyer has pointed it out in one of his talks that we have to stop putting into our body, substances that are detrimental to it, if we really wish to experience higher consciousness levels. When you are addicted to something, you are basically experiencing the same old pain again and again. Your consciousness does not expand, it starts stinking because of the stagnancy. As spiritual beings having a human experience, our job is to evolve and stay fresh and that can happen only by learning something new and dying to the old. When you repeat an addictive behavior, you are basically repeating your life. It's like playing the same track again and again. Even if it is your favorite song, how many times can you listen to it? Repetition brings boredom into life. It makes life tasteless and dull. Change is the spice of life and you can invite it by transcending your addictions.

Addictions can paralyze the mind by creating an imaginary perimeter around it. Every time the mind tries to jump across that circumference, the elastic band of withdrawal symptoms and the history of your defeats pull you back. You are mentally incapacitated by the control that an addiction exercises over your mind. You are no longer the master of your destiny; you become a slave of your habits. Once the elephant of our mind has been chained for a period long enough, you can tie it with a thread and it won't try to break free. The making up of our mind is such that if it has been enslaved for too long, it stops thinking about freedom. That was the reason why India got used to foreign rules and that is the reason why each one of us has a hard time dealing with his or her addictions.

Every addiction has got a vicious cycle of its own that becomes a psychological jail for you. If someone takes L.S.D. once every month, he is not an addict, he is just an experimenter. But if he starts taking it on the 1st of every month, the thing has started exercising its hold upon him. When you find yourself compelled into doing things that do not synchronize with your highest values, you have fallen prey to them. Once the clock of an addiction has forced you into surrender, it will use you like a servant to maintain itself. The wise ones have remarked, "Mind is great as a slave but terrible as a master." When the withdrawal symptoms make you run for your addiction, it has established its throne in your mind and conquered you. Now obviously, it will take you a rebellion to do something about an occupied throne.

We all know that our brain produces secretions that decide our emotions. In a healthy person, all these secretions are in a perfect harmony. But when we get addicted to a substance that has got chemicals which produce certain emotions, our emotions are no longer in harmony with the rest of our being. Even if you are happy, optimistic, energetic or ecstatic, it is all synthetic and unnatural. It has not come out of you naturally like spring water; you have forced it out. Because of this lack of harmony between your different moods, because of this emotional imbalance, you become unpredictable, impulsive, indecisive and fluctuating. Our mind is in fact one of the most complex creations of god and it is something to be used and explored, not something to be played with recklessly. If you explore the mind, it could open the doors to liberation. But if you play with it carelessly, the consequences could be complicating, even fatal.

An addiction can also teach you procrastination. You try to postpone all decision-making and effort making because your primary focus is to stay the way you are. They also call it the comfort zone. You want to stay close to your comfort without being aware of how much discomfort it may be sowing for you to reap in the future. You are unable to see that you are offering months and years at the altar of your mornings and evenings. By clinging to the smaller picture, you are ignoring the bigger view of your precious incarnation. All your change and effort making is saved for some hypothetical tomorrow while your today keeps on stinking.

Addictions make you a dependent. You are unable to do without them. Sages have defined three levels of maturity of a soul; the first level is dependence, the second is independence and the third is interdependence. So an addiction basically keeps your soul stuck at the first level of maturity. When you are unable to stand on your own, you are compelled into leaning on others. In a mysterious way, the remote control of your life lands into the hands of others. And others are others. They may decide to do nothing about you and let you just rot away. Or they may decide to exploit you in a thousand different ways. Just remember that where there is dependence, there is exploitation; where there is love; there is liberty. Dependence makes you vulnerable and open to manipulation and politics of the minds of others.

Addictions encourage the escapist in all of us. Instead of solving a problem, we start avoiding its sight by choosing temporary reliefs and keeping our thinking the same. Albert Einstein offers us a great insight when he says, "You can never solve a problem with the same thinking that produced it." Our problems do not wait for us to make a decision to solve them; they keep on growing in size. Therefore, it's wise to do something about them while they are minor. But, with our self esteem lowered, our body, mind and soul weakened and our connectivity with our own greatness blocked, we develop a tendency to run away from challenges. So, in a way, our addictions become magnets that attract problems and keep on heaping them for us to deal with. Mr. Anthony Robbins has done a great research into our tendencies to escape from the challenges of life and all the ways in which we sabotage ourselves. Challenges are for, "Living up to", they are not for, "Escaping From."

People who get addicted to drugs, alcohol, opium and the like are most of the time worried about running out of their stock because it is not something easily available at grocery shops. This concern becomes a thick wall between them and the "Isness" of the existence. Every experience of theirs gets diluted by the future and they miss the celebration contained within small events of life. Heavy doses of such stuff can make you insensitive to the subtleness of life and you require some thick kind of happiness. Your mind stops responding to the miracles of ordinary living. It is a great spiritual handicap. It is as if you are surrounded by an ocean but can't drink from it.

Over a period of years, an addiction can also make you a pleasure seeker. Now, there is nothing wrong in looking for pleasure but when you refuse to take the other side of that coin which is pain, you are, in a way, trying to pass life through a filter. In your running away from it and not wanting it, your pain actually increases. There is a time to be happy and there is a time to be sad. You cannot break life into pieces, keep the ones you like and throw away the ones you don't. Life comes in the form of a complete package. You can take it or leave it. You can't make choices. You cannot create another kind of a life. You can only understand the one that has been given to you and then evolve it to its highest glory. You can start with its mortal half and then rise up to its immortality. Addictions can keep you stuck in its mortal part because no matter what you experience by using external substances, those experiences have only been induced; they have not yet been achieved by you. It takes decades to taste the real thing and for that, pain has to be embraced. In your case, the first pain to be embraced would be, jumping out of your addiction.

I have tried my best to bring to your notice the alarming aspect of being addicted to something in a negative way. If that was enough, then you are standing at a point where you are going to make one of the most crucial decisions of your life - The decision to becoming addiction free. If you would like to know what a real decision looks like then here are a few quotations from some of the greatest achievers.

1) A real decision is measured by the fact that you have taken a new action. If there's no action, you haven't truly decided.

Tony Robbins

2) It is in your moments of decision that your destiny is shaped.

Tony Robbins

3)The best way to predict your future is to create it.

Anonymous

4) Once a decision has been made you should close your ears to even the best counter argument; this is the sign of a strong character.

Anonymous

5) Using the power of decision gives you the capacity to change any and every part of your life in an instant.

Tony Robbins.

6) Once you make a decision, the entire universe conspires to make it happen.

Ralph Waldo Emerson

Part 2

Breaking Free Of An Addiction

In the first chapter, I tried to bring to your notice, how your addictions are something you cannot afford to ignore even for one more day. In this chapter I will try to explain how they become a blessing in disguise the moment you decide to step out of them. The moment you decide to change, the whole scenario changes. It is one of those paradoxes of life where you come to understand that hidden inside every misery, are the seeds of bliss. Once your addiction is something of the past, you can convert it into your most valuable source of insight into your own self. It can be your personnel Veda. It can lay down the foundation for the flowering of your soul.

The first thing you do for becoming addiction free is the one suggested by Dr. Wayne Dyer and that is - "Love your addictions." Don't hate them. There is a great secret in that. When you bring love into any situation, the results can be miraculous. The whole situation starts moving in a different direction. By inviting love, you create an atmosphere in which miracles can happen and every change that you bring about in your life is a small miracle. Love opens up the situation to a realm in which nothing is impossible and provides you with an access to the infinite power of God. For a man of faith becoming addiction free is just as easy as it was to become an addict.

The next thing on your agenda should be replacing your identity of an addict with that of someone who is free of addiction. This is very important. Our mind always precedes our manifested life. Unless you do something in your thoughts, it is very difficult to manifest it on the material plane of reality. It takes only 20 days to free yourself of an addiction, but it can take you 20 years to make the decision to do so. And what is a decision? It is just a thought. It is just something in your mind. It is just a plan that is waiting to be executed. So when you think about yourself, visualize yourself as someone who is addiction free. The substance of your addiction should simply not be there in your image. The world that you create for yourself follows your thoughts like a shadow. Used correctly, your mind assists you in moving towards the most peaceful outcomes. It becomes your friend.

The identity of an addict is a part of your sense of self - your ego. No one ever says, "My body and my mind are addicted to this or that." We always say, "I am addicted to this thing." Now, who is this I? It is your sense of your self – it is your ego. And who is the one who wishes to end up all this suffering and come out of it? It is the one who knows that it has got the potential to do so - it is your consciousness; the anchor of God in you. On the surface it appears that the battle of addiction is between you and the substance you are addicted to, but if you go deep into it, you will find that the battle is actually between your awareness and the combination of your mind and your ego. In the survival of the addict, your entire ego survives but in its elimination, a part of it gets eliminated. So the ego tries to cling to an addiction while the awareness tries to pull you out of it.

From the day you decide to quit something to the day you are absolutely clean, you must stay away from your sense of self – your ego because as soon as we move into it, we become unconscious. Rest in awareness and be on the alert all day. Don't slip into your identity. We do that every day. We deliberately abandon our consciousness and slip into unconsciousness because we know that it is not possible for us to be aware and to do something we are not supposed to do. We enjoy our trip, then move back into awareness and feel guilty about it. It's an old game and we have become masters at deceiving ourselves by playing it so frequently. We choose to forget because remembering needs strength. We choose to forget and slip into the automatic patterns of the ego to avoid the responsibility that comes with staying on guard. Why would someone sit all night in front of a gate with a rifle in his hand when he has got the choice to slip into a bed? Only if the thing being guarded is precious enough. Isn't your incarnation precious?

There's another method of freeing yourself of addiction in which you use the ego itself and this is for those who have not yet created enough awareness or the space of the witness. In this method, you do it for a triumph, a victory. Instead of holding on to the witness, here you hold on to your sense of triumph and fight against your addiction like a warrior. People who have a very great desire for victory over something can go for this method. Though I won't be discussing too much of it; the reason being I don't want to liberate you from one thing and get you trapped into another. But if you wish to go for this, then I would recommend someone who is really an Ustad (expert) in it - Mr. Anthony Robbins. He is one of the very few who have made a tremendous effort in getting to know the mechanics of the mind. Even those who want to use awareness as their principle tool can still use their ego as a vehicle and make things easier for themselves. The pain of having to give up addiction can be negated by the pleasure of becoming addiction free and victory over addiction can serve as a boost for the ego.

When you have tried to give up something several times and you have failed to do so, a loser becomes an integral part of your identity. Every failed attempt thickens the looser and reinforces the addiction. The taste of transcendence remains unknown to you and defeat becomes a familiar thought pattern of your mind. But why are you defeated? Since there is no enemy out there, it must be that you have learnt some self defeating ways. You are defeated because you add your consciousness to the loser in you. You add your soul to your ego; the ego of someone who has surrendered to the withdrawal symptoms of an addiction. You provide all your energy to the loser in you and convert that simple obstacle of addiction into a china wall; a mere difficulty into an impossibility. Pull away your energy and those self-defeating thought patterns will automatically collapse. They will stop like a vehicle that has run out of fuel.

I have designed a 21 days (3 Weeks) programme to assist you in giving up an addiction. If it is too short, your body and mind are unable to cope with the change; if it is extended too much, it could be interrupted by your worldly responsibilities. In the first week we go for a complete fast. In the second and third week we stay on restricted diet. You can stay on restricted diet for a longer duration if you feel the need to do so. Your individuality has to be taken into account while going on with any programme. But before going for the fast, you are required to have cut down the intake of your substance of addiction to at least half and if possible one third of the usual amount. Because when we go for a fast, it gets cut down to zero and can be a bit shocking for your metabolism. Throughout the programme, we stay on guard and observe the whole happening from the dimension of awareness, the space of the witness. We stay rooted and then pull our body and mind out of their conditioning. We stay there and remind ourselves as many times as we have to that we are neither the body nor the mind, we are neither the emotions nor the sense of "I"; we are pure consciousness.

I am sure you have been making adjustments in your life to suit your addiction. Now make a few to suit your breaking free of it. Avoid any commitments that can be taxing for you. Staying aware is in itself a tough job and takes a lot of your energy as long as it has not become your permanent residence. Save all your energy for the task at hand. Make changes in your diet (What you eat) so that it synchronizes with your programme. Don't take heavy stuff, don't take foods and drinks that affect the emptying of your bowels in any way and don't take anything which you know from experience, is not good for you. Keep everything simple and easy. Include an hour of meditation in your routine. It will help you stay rooted in awareness.

We will be starting our de-addiction programme with a fast of one week. But if you are very thin and already underweight, you can skip this and move on to the next part of our programme which is restricted diet. If you can afford, go for a 3 days fast and then move on. But those who are overweight or even normal must go for a one week fast in which you do not take anything other than lemon juice or orange juice. You can add some salt if you feel like but no sugar. Honey can be added for better cleansing, but not much, because of the heat it produces. Now, fasting helps us in achieving three major goals. The first is the detoxifying of our body, the second is the breaking of the thought patterns of our addiction and the third is regaining control over our self. I will try my best to explain each of them in detail.

Fasting detoxifies our body of all the toxins we have accumulated over the years or maybe decades. Wastes that are almost a poison for our body can be thrown out of it only by a religious fast. When there is nothing to digest and assimilate, our metabolism starts working on the substances deposited in the depth of our tissues. Many of our ailments are because of these unwanted elements in the layers of our physical being. Our daily doses of our addiction are not the only cause of our withdrawal symptoms; it is the reserve stuff stored in our body that tends to maintain itself on a certain level. When you quit an addiction, the cravings are more severe when the body has run out of its reserve stock than when it has been cut off from the regular supply. A fast carries out a deep cleansing of our metabolism in addition to offering it a badly needed rest from the daily digestions, assimilations and transportations. Rest is the only way to re-energize an exhausted part of this existence. A fast is for the digestive system, what a sleep is for the body and enlightenment is for the soul.

A fast provides your metabolism with the time required to switch from an addiction to normalcy. It's a big change and should be made tenderly, not harshly. All the secretions that were being forced out of your system by external stimulants will now have to be produced by the body in a more natural way. All the emotional kick and punch you got from your substance of addiction will be replaced by a uniformity and stability of moods. Water and the purifying agents assist our body in making this shift. Lemon is the king of cleansing in naturopathy and honey makes it all the more effective. Together they can extract impurities from the depths of our organs and remind our body of its miraculous ability to heal itself of all ailments and afflictions.

If we look at our addictions from a psychological angle, they are patterns of thoughts that have become a part of our being and almost automatic because of us having lived with them for so long. Fasting interrupts these patterns in the most efficient way. It throws the vicious cycle of addiction out of your daily routine and creates for you a life that is pure and natural; not a chemically driven one. There are billions of us following the clock of addiction without being aware of it. We are unaware of this clock because we have never ever stepped out of it. When things are too close to us they can go totally unobserved. Fasting pulls out all the needles of this clock and gives you a glimpse of the gap between moments, the living freshness behind our dead automatic routines. If we do not go for a complete fast and just cut down on the amount of our daily intake of an addiction, the patterns of the mind are not destroyed, they keep on existing.

Those who get addicted to caffeine and nicotine are unable to empty their bowels without an early morning dose of their addiction. So, in their case, the addiction establishes its hold upon the metabolism in the form of emptying of the bowels. Every addiction has its own way to establish such hold and to impose itself on our daily routine. This imposition can be best tackled by a fast. A fast leaves no space for the exploitation of your metabolism. When there is nothing to do, you do not need anything to do it with. The cycle of addiction runs out of its convincing power when you rob it of all the excuses for its maintenance. This is very important because the greatest obstacle to getting rid of an addiction is the cycle of addiction or the clock of addiction which we adhere to, for decades and sometimes, lifetimes.

The physical weakness felt during a fast makes you aware of your energy body. Your energy level is so low that it becomes the focus of your attention. Even a light physical effort such as walking a few steps can leave you depleted of energy. This awareness of something in you that cannot be seen brings you closer to the dimension from where you can look at the patterns of an addiction and it is this looking at these patterns that is going to set you free of them once and for all. The nature of spirituality is such that as soon as you can see something, you are liberated from it. If you can see your lust, anger, greed, attachment and ego, addiction is not a very big deal. It is only a lack of consciousness that can be exploited by the lure of an addiction. Such impermanent pleasures cannot be sold to the awakened.

The only exercise that I would recommend to you during the one week fast is, mindful breathing. Just watch the pendulum of your breath moving to and fro between your abdomen and your nostrils. When your abdomen rises, you breathe in; when it falls, you breathe out. The decision to watch the rising and falling of the abdomen and the pendulum of breath is made by the mind. But after some time, the mind steps aside and you shift into the dimension of pure consciousness. The mind gets out of your way because there is nothing much to think about. What possibly can you think about something as simple as the rising and falling of an abdomen? This simple exercise is more powerful and effective than it appears to be. It is the shortest shortcut to awareness and witnessing. People have underestimated its effectiveness because of its simplicity and plainness. We are used to things that are complex and sophisticated. This practice has the potential to keep you firmly rooted in awareness and not get carried away by the winds of emotions.

As I mentioned, the first task of a fast is to detoxify your body and the second is to destroy the patterns of an addiction. The third task is to assist you in regaining your control over yourself because the presence of an addiction in your life clearly indicates a lack of self-control. If you are taking something that is not good for you, on a daily basis, it leaves no doubt about the fact that there is still a corner in your being which has escaped the illumination of your wisdom. It is possible to be highly conscious in one aspect of your being while another one totally misses your attention. Scientists and spiritualists are often so lost in their work that they are unable to give their physical health the attention it needs. Our life asks for a frequent scanning with the torch of wisdom so that there are no dark corners left in our being. That which can be seen is just as important as that which cannot be. Without this body, how could we live the life that is there to be lived? Without these eyes how could we see the mystery that surrounds us? Without these ears how could we listen to the music everywhere? Without this tongue how could we taste the flavors of life? Without these hands how could we touch the ones we love? The madness of chase has robbed all of us of the wonders that were given to us by the existence free of cost. Have we ever paid for a sunrise and a sunset? Have we ever paid for the dawn and the dusk? Can we buy a beautiful child with all our wealth put together? Have we ever spent a day in gratitude; feeling grateful for all that has been showered upon us? The chase of mankind is a madness and when this madness creeps into us, we lose control over ourselves.

When you are on a fast, the desire for food becomes very thick and to say "No" to that desire, your awareness also has to be equally thick. Every time the desire springs up, you have to push yourself away from it and seek refuge in pure consciousness. You cannot trust the mind because it can easily convince you into breaking a fast. For the first time, after a long history of an addictive behavior, you are very acutely aware of the level on which this game is being played. There is this nagging desire for food, there is this mind that cannot be trusted and there is this consciousness that can provide you with the strength to carry on with your programme. This ability to watch everything so clearly is exactly the one that is required to break free of an addiction. The lack of it results in lack of self control. The basic pattern of an addiction can be reduced to a desire that wants to be fulfilled, a mind that gets convinced and a "You" that steps down from the throne of consciousness to join the other two. Self control is, staying on that throne, refusing to step down and watching from there the rest of your being playing those old tricks with you.

During the one week fast, make sure that you make an effort to empty your bowels, at least for 20-30 minutes every morning. This will keep your excretory system toned up and not let it become inactive. A good emptying of the bowels plays a great role in the cleansing of the body and our system responds best to a routine effort and a healthy diet. Diarrhea and constipation can be one of the withdrawal symptoms when you are on a de-addiction programme. But they don't stay there forever if they are just allowed to be and not exaggerated by your mind. A regular sitting on the toilet seat makes it easier for you to return to normalcy when you come out of the fast and start taking solid food. But don't take any medicine for this because more than 90% of them are habit forming and are an addiction for the bowels. The purpose of the fast is not only to get the substance of your addiction out of your body but to help you heal of all ailments - known and unknown.

Now let us see what withdrawal symptoms are and how we are going to handle them since they are going to be most intense during the first week. Withdrawal symptoms are simply an indication that our whole being is going through a change. Whether it is a headache, nausea, an upset stomach or an upset mood, it is nothing but your being expressing its discomfort due to the change you have decided to make. Some unease is always associated with every change we make in our lives and we have to embrace it in order to grow. If we don't do so, we have to settle down for the pain of stagnancy and deterioration. There is great wisdom in allowing change and impermanence into your life; there is no wisdom in clinging and decaying. The withdrawal symptoms of an addiction are simply indications of a transition; they are not some emergency to be dealt with. They are not your body screaming for help; they are your body adapting to change. If you can watch them from the dimension of awareness, they can be a blessing in disguise; they can free you from your identification with the body and its discomforts.

What's crucial for you to know is that the real problem is not with the symptom itself; the real problem is the pattern of the mind this particular symptom triggers. Suppose someone is addicted to caffeine. The moment a craving springs up in the person's body for caffeine, he or she starts making a cup of coffee or tea. When this pattern is repeated day after day, month after month, year after year, it gets engraved on the mind like an engraving on stone. When you are freeing yourself of an addiction, you have to stay on guard and stay away from this pattern so that it can self- destruct. The cravings of the body and the mind are a trap for your consciousness; they are a false alarm that the body and the mind use to resist change. Be aware of them. Let the old patterns of the mind perish to create space for new ones. Let change be accepted and absorbed by every part of your being. Every time a discomfort arises because of the change you are making, remind yourself of all the pain and suffering that you have gone through in the past because of your clinging. Let that suffering be the driving force behind your persistence and your commitment to this de-addiction programme.

The first weak is going to be tough. You will be dealing with physical weakness due to fasting on one hand and the withdrawal symptoms on the other hand. But everything will take care of itself if you just stay rooted in awareness. Think about this pain just the way a mother thinks about her labor pains in order to bring a beautiful child into this world. Think about the fruits of your labor, the freedom that will come from it and the growth that will become a permanent part of your consciousness. Think about the change you can make in this world with your own transformation. Think about those that you can liberate, once you are liberated yourself. Think about the amount of suffering you could eliminate once you have reached the dimension from where you have a complete understanding of human pain. Stay connected to the infinite power and unlimited endurance of pure consciousness.

During the fast, the mind will try to interfere in your affairs with all kinds of rationalizations. You will have to stay on guard and keep it simple and straight. The purpose of the fast is not only to cleanse the body and destroy the patterns of addiction; it is also to tame the mind and to not let it interfere in matters that are beyond its realm. The mind will say, "If you can have lemon juice and orange juice then there should be no problem with having all the fruit juices and even vegetable soups." The mind will say, "Seven days are a bit too much; 3 to 4 days should be enough." The mind will say, "What's the point in living a life that is so dull and tasteless?" the mind will keep on disturbing you with its logical and rational explanations but we are here to move beyond these practicalities of the mind, into a dimension where you can exist and relate with life without thinking; where thinking is not necessary to process life. Addiction to a substance is only one of the ways in which the clinging of the mind surfaces in our life. The real problem is our lack of an understanding of the nature of the mind.

After a religious fast of one week, you should move on to restricted diet and stay there for as many weeks as you find necessary, for the change that you have made, to become an integral part of your being. The change should be permanent. There should not be even a 1% chance of you going back to your old ways. We are not here to play some hide and seek with our addictions; we are here to step out of all such deteriorations once and for all. By designing this programme for you, I have tried to assist you in regaining control over yourself through exercising control over the decisions you make in the space that exists between a stimulus and a response. In this case, the stimulus is the desire for food and the response is your eating habits. We are going to tackle addiction from a completely unexpected angle. If we can conquer this space, we can conquer our self. That does not mean everything in the outside world will happen exactly the way we want it to, but we will surely be able to live a disciplined and religious life within the framework of the society and our incarnation.

Break your one week fast with a small serving of rice and then follow the regimen of restricted diet. In this regimen you will be having four small meals per day and the size of your meal should be almost half the size of what you used to eat at one sitting before you began this de-addiction programme. Two of your meals should be rich in carbohydrates and two should be rich in proteins. Don't worry about the minerals and multivitamins. There will be some in every diet. Take a glass of lemon juice (Juice of one lemon + a glass of water) in the morning to continue the cleansing of the body and keep everything as simple as you can. I will explain the logic behind this diet schedule so that you have an understanding of what we are trying to accomplish.

Addiction is basically a form of attachment and food is one area of our life where our attachment exhibits itself in the most noticeable fashion. If we can exercise control over our eating habits, we can exercise control over our attachment to anything; with some persistent effort, of course. This is why you need to cut down on the quantity of your meal. I have personally observed that almost all of us overeat. We don't stop at the minimum that is enough; we stop at the maximum that can be digested. We eat every meal as if it were our last meal. We ignore the simple truth that our body can absorb only a certain amount of the nutrients in one go. The rest is a liability for the digestive system and of absolutely no positive value. A professional bodybuilder knows this and makes most of his gains by practicing this principle. All his success depends upon how well he can use the laws of his metabolism to his advantage. We can all use these laws to eat sensibly and live a healthy life.

Now, eating a small meal doesn't mean you cannot derive from it, the pleasure that you used to. By eating meditatively and diving into the depths of the tastes and flavors of your meal, you will feel absolutely gratified at the end of it. A small meal will provide you with energy while a big one will give you lethargy. When you chew your food well and it leaves you energetic and nourished, you realize that there is god in that food and it is something to be treated with respect. A nice way of putting it is that you should "Drink the solids and eat the liquids"; which implies that the solid food should be chewed so well that it becomes a liquid and the liquid foods should be sipped so slowly that you appear to be eating them.

I have designed a simple diet menu for you so that you can have an exact idea of the way things are going to be, in actual.

9 am - Cheese/ milk/sprouts

1 pm - Small meal (Brown bread/Rice/Cereal)

5 pm - Cheese/milk/2 bananas/2 mangoes

9 pm - Small meal (Brown bread/Rice/Cereal)

I have tried to keep it simple so that it can be easily put to practice. You can design your own menus and then stick to them religiously. Now to go on with this plan every meal of yours should be just as much as can be easily digested within 3 hours. The purpose of this plan is not to make you a Mr. Olympia; it is just to help you tame your desires and establish yourself as the master of your mind.

Meditate for about 5 minutes before every meal and try to listen to your body in order to know what it needs. We usually impose our choices on our belly and our choices are based upon the look and taste of a food, not its food value. Taste can be used to choose the right food provided we don't manipulate our intuition. Listening to the body means, silencing our cravings for all the tempting stuff that is there to eat and drink and allowing our body to decide what's best for it. It is an art that you will be able to master after some sincere practice and it will help you in cultivating a very pious relationship with food. The food that the body asks for is a medicine for it whereas the food that you push down your throat on the basis of your taste buds could be a poison for it. Your taste buds can be your friend or enemy depending upon how you use them. If used wisely, they can bridge the gap between you and your awareness; if used unwisely, they could be the cause of the downfall of your health.

The reason behind emphasizing so much on meditative eating is to ensure that you have to discipline yourself at least five to six times every day because it is due to the lack of such a discipline or self control that you have lived the life of an addict and suffered. Now, self-control does not mean that you tighten yourself up with dead rituals and fixed routines. It simply means that you have the capacity to push yourself away from your body as well as your mind and seek refuge in a dimension that is beyond the reach of the mind and its clinging. True discipline can only flower in this dimension;

all other disciplines are merely a vehicle to reach here. In your case, we are using food as a vehicle to step out of the mind. Your addiction was a brainchild of your mind. So it is the mind that is the root of all your suffering and it is the mind that needs your attention, not its sophisticated manifestations. The divine purpose of your addiction was to enable you to see the root cause of all your suffering. The day this insight blooms in your consciousness, you will have no negative feelings for the life you lived as an addict. You will love your addictions though you won't be addicted to them anymore.

Since you are taking four meals every day, you can add a light physical workout to your routine. The best would be something you have never tried before. It will assist you in adding strength to your new identity. It could be a walk, swimming, yoga, aerobics, Tai Chi or anything that gives your body a break from its stationary jobs. It will maintain the flow of your energy and protect the vitality of your organs. The mindful breathing I mentioned earlier, is to be continued and if possible, you should add to it, breathing exercises from yoga. These breathing exercises will not only supply oxygen to the ignored parts of your body, they will separate you from your identification with the body the way the pulp of a ripe coconut is separated from its shell.

Throughout the fast and the restricted diet, you will have to keep an eye on the resistance that your old identity exhibits against change and discipline. You know the truth of the saying, "Old habits die hard." This whole programme is to consciously watch them die. Tenaciously, hold on to your new identity. If your suffering has been very heavy and thick, this change is going to feel like a re-incarnation. You will be throwing a lot of unwanted things away from you and creating a space for new ones. A great poet has said in one of his works, "The old order changes yielding place to new; lest one custom should corrupt the world." His words contain the essence of change and impermanence. So don't deny change, don't run away from it, don't try to do something about the discomfort that accompanies it and don't be alarmed by the strange feeling it creates in you. Stay a witness to it and allow it to be absorbed by your consciousness. When it has been absorbed, it will become your wisdom, your growth, your insight, your endurance and your strength. It is like the manure, which when absorbed by the plant, blooms into a beautiful flower.

Chapter 7 – FEAR

There is no fear in the eyes of a new born baby; only curiosity. There is no curiosity in the eyes of an old man; only fear. Between these two extremes, the whole world exists. We first learn to be afraid, then condition that learning and after a few decades fear becomes the most fundamental "Mantra" recited by our soul in the background of its peripheral existence in this world. The unpredicted blows of fate eat away our trust in life like a termite and our subconscious mind is always trembling because of its belief in the probability of a crocodile in every lake that appears to be calm on the surface. Our fear is not illogical or irrational; it has got its roots in our first hand experiences of life and those experiences could even be from some past incarnation of ours. The wound heals; the scar remains. Our fear is the sum-total of all such scars.

Once you come across a snake in a lawn, your trust in that grass is shattered. Once you have been let down by someone you were emotionally very attached to, your trust in the warmth of relationships is gone. The survivors of shark attacks have a very hard time going back to the ocean again; the ocean that used to be their very soul. Fear is instilled into us by our own experiences; it does not show up from nowhere. How much trust in life can you expect from a child who has lost his or her parents in a riot, partition, accident or war? How much trust in relationships can you expect from the children of divorced parents who have spent all their childhood in foster homes? A new born baby has as much faith in this existence as the Christ. The absence of that faith is fear. It is that kid's curiosity that has been shattered to pieces.

Let us see what some of the greatest fears are, the ones which are robbing all of us of our peace of mind. There is this fear of death, there is the fear of our marriage falling apart, there is the fear of poverty, there is the fear of sickness, there is the fear of harm to our children, there is the fear of loss of our loved ones, there is the fear of harm to our social status and our image in the society, there is the fear of a mass destruction or a global disaster, there is the fear of a major financial loss or setback and there is the fear of a physical, emotional or political assault by those who consider themselves our enemies. These are the major ones. There are many more minor fears lurking in the corners of our subconscious mind and unless and until we consciously explore this part of our being, there is no way to get rid of them.

We feed our fears without being aware of it. We never make an effort to dispel them with our wisdom and awareness; we are always busy adding our negativity to them and making them grow bigger and bigger. We never try to look at our fears and trace their origin; we just go on trembling at their sight and allow them to dictate our life and dominate our being. There is no doubt about the fact that all our fears are, to some extent, logical and rational but there is also no doubt about the fact that they can all be logically and rationally dissolved. For example, you can live for years fearing that you are suffering from AIDS or cancer but you can dissolve that fear in a single day by getting a few clinical tests done. If you look into the depth of such a fear you will be surprised that it comes from a day in your past when you were informed by a doctor that you are suffering from a life threatening disease. It could have happened 20 years ago but the scar is still there. Every fear of ours has got a root and an origin. Our job is to find it and dispel it.

If I had drowned in some previous incarnation of mine, I would obviously be afraid of water. The sight of a lake, river, canal or pool will remind my soul of the potential of this liquid to kill someone. In a way, because of a horrible experience of mine, water has got associated with death. So, wherever I see it in large quantity, I would see death. It would be an absolutely natural fear. Now, how can I dispel it? - By learning to swim and then becoming a great swimmer. You can apply this technique of handling fear to any of your fears. It will work each and every time without fail. It will definitely take some time to convert a fear into a faith, but it is not something that cannot be accomplished. If we were born without fear, we can live without fear. If we have lost a faith, we can find it too. All that is required is a dedication and persistence.

Our fears are paths that can lead us to our subconscious mind; the one that designs all our dreams. Our dreams can also tell us a lot about those layers of our being that lie beneath the obvious. A fear should always be tracked right to its origin so that it can be uprooted from the soul. And don't be surprised if that origin turns out to be your mother's womb itself. If you were not even born yet and your mother lost someone very dear to her or met with an accident, the fear of death could have been instilled into you right there. The thought patterns of a parent can leave long lasting impressions on the mind of a child and most of us are very careless in handling this fact. A balanced diet is not enough for a carrying woman. If she wants to give birth to a child of faith, she must feed on faith, not fear.

Every fear is a resistance to the divine will and exhibits lack of faith. When a father stands at the edge of the roof top of a 30 storey building with his six months old baby in his arms and they both look down from there, the baby shows absolutely no signs of a panic and feels totally safe in its parent's arms; the two small feet of God dangling playfully. That's faith. We are all children of God and ought to trust our parent. With our fears and panics, we are basically demonstrating that we do not trust the divine will. This lack of faith becomes a distance between us and God; it separates us from our parent's love and leaves us feeling insecure and unloved.

There's this story of an enlightened being known for his weird methods of making people aware of themselves. One day, he decided to find out, how much of faith one of his disciples had in him. So, in the middle of the night, he approached the sleeping disciple with a dagger in his hand, jumped over him and sat on his chest with the blade touching the young man's throat. The disciple woke up startled at this sudden assault on him and at such an odd hour, but as soon as he discovered that it was his master, he closed his eyes and made no attempt to save himself or fight back. The master made a small cut with the tip of the dagger; the disciple still stayed calm. The master got up and walked away, with a satisfaction he had not had in years. The next morning the commune followed their daily routine and so did the disciple, showing absolutely no signs of shock or disturbance. The master called him by his side and asked the student, "When you saw me in that weird form weren't you afraid?" "I trust you Master and I am absolutely sure that whatever you will do to me will be for my good", the disciple replied. Life often sits on our chest with a blade touching our throat and we have only two options to choose from; fear or faith. The choice we make decides our religiousness; our spirituality.

Unless we replace fear with faith, we cannot enter into the dimension which Jesus called "The Kingdom of God". With your fear, you are not allowing your soul to expand beyond a certain measure and this boundary becomes the separation between you and the ocean of life you are surrounded by. It is as if a bottle containing water is floating in an ocean of water. The water inside the bottle remains cut off from the ocean due to its container. Fear does not let us know the taste of faith. There are forces that come into play only when you invite them. If you are going away from home for a few days and you trust the existence to take care of your family, there are forces that will live up to your faith. But if you are afraid; the results will be different. Not because there was nothing to handle things in your absence, but because you did not have faith in it. You can either invite the existence with your faith or you can invite negative events with your fear. Those negative events are also a part of the existence but they are certainly not liberating for you and they are not what you want for yourself.

There is a life beyond fear which will never become known to those who are living in fear. The "Man of faith" may look like any other human being but the life he lives belongs to, a totally different space. He is in communion with laws and forces that are beyond the comprehension of someone who is living in fear. Faith opens the gates of your being to the infinite. When a child shows trust in its parent, the parent becomes all the more responsible, not careless. The faith of the child becomes a sacred expectation that the parent has to live up-to. When the child looks at its parent with two innocent eyes full of hope, the parent makes a thousand changes to accommodate that hope and to protect it from shattering. In the same way, when a man of faith entrusts this existence with the task of protecting him and stands in prayer with hope in his eyes, the existence moves a thousand pieces around to accommodate his religiousness.

The gambler, who wins every-time at a game where he had equal chances to lose, has got more faith than the so called religious person who attracts in his life, all that he does not want. If things that you do not want, keep on showing up in your life, it is a clear indication that fear is dominating your being and steering the boat of your incarnation. The "Man of faith" is the greatest gambler of all. He can emerge victorious from situations where his very life is at stake. We all know about people who suffered from life threatening diseases like cancer and restored themselves to health with the sheer power of their faith. They could have easily lost that battle and offered all their energies in the service of the sickness. But they did not give up and held on to the possibility of a miracle. And where there is faith, there are miracles. Faith is the soil on which the flowers of miracles grow.

Always keep this in your mind that wherever there is fear, there is an opportunity to know faith. Faith is a knowing, an experience; it is not just a wishful thinking. I will use cancer as an example because I find so many of my fellow beings standing face to face with that life threatening disease. The moment someone discovers that he or she is suffering from it, there are only two options to choose from; the fear of death or the faith in a miracle. Now, cancer is not the bite of a king cobra that you don't have the time to save yourself; it is just a few unhealthy cells. Your faith can stop their growth; your fear can make them multiply. What would you get by choosing fear? And people do that. They offer more than 90% of their being in the service of a few cells who have earned a bad name by getting associated with death. But the ones who choose faith are not only cured, they are reincarnated and they start living from a space that doesn't even belong to the ordinary world. They have discovered the anchor of God in their own being and come to know their true potential.

Fear always thinks in terms of all that can possibly go wrong where as faith believes that nothing is impossible for God and for those who have succeeded in establishing a communion with the infinity. Fear is a spiritual handicap. It cuts you off from your true potential with a self created barrier, a self imposed limitation. The freedom from every fear lies in learning to handle the object you are afraid of. If you are afraid of water, your freedom will come from learning how to swim. If you are afraid of snakes, your freedom lies in learning how to handle snakes. If you are afraid of height, your freedom lies in bungee jumping. If you are afraid of death, your freedom will come from conscious death or dying while you are alive. If you are afraid of your spouse taking advantage of the liberty you offer to him or her, your freedom will come from making him or her responsible for his or her Karma and distancing yourself from his or her decisions, mistakes and suffering, without being uncompassionate. If you are afraid of your enemies, your freedom will come from accommodating them in your being, accepting them as a part of the divine will and dealing with them with no hatred in your heart. Whatever you are afraid of contains an opportunity of discovering the life that exists beyond fear.

The divine purpose of fear is to protect you from a potential harm by alerting you to it. If you don't know how to swim and you jump into a river, unless you are someone with supernatural powers, you are most probably going to drown. Fear warns you well in advance and wakes you up to the reality of a situation so that you don't act recklessly. In adequate amounts, it is a friend not a foe. If there is a king cobra in front of you, fear will tell you not to make an unintelligent move. If you are driving rashly, fear will remind you that "Speed thrills but kills". If your anger has become very explosive, fear will make you exercise self-control by giving you a glimpse of what your anger can lead you to. If there were no such thing as fear, we would frequently walk into dangers. It is only when our fear grows out of proportion that it loses its utility and defeats its own purpose. Most of our fears grow into phobias if cultivated for too long and it is these phobias that we need to free ourselves from. When every rope in the dark starts looking like a snake, we need to do something about it.

Now whenever someone is going through some kind of suffering, some kind of pain, our natural inclination is to move away from that pain for the fear of getting entangled in it. But we ultimately get entangled in the avoidance of pain. From his own experiences, Shri Ram Dass had a great insight that to be freed of suffering, you have to move towards it, not away from it. The fear of our own anticipated suffering and the real suffering of others is more than the suffering itself. The suffering is always in the "Now" but the fear expands to the left and right of that "Now' and with the fear, the suffering also starts expanding. The energy of fear exaggerates every problem and throws you out of the space from where it can be solved. But when you move towards a suffering, accept that suffering and embrace that suffering, you discover the other side of that coin – the oneness behind dualities. Living in fear implies living a limb of life and being cut off from the wholeness of it. The fear of suffering deprives you of the wisdom of suffering or the understanding of suffering and without an understanding of your own suffering and the suffering of others, you cannot taste or touch the dimension of compassion; the space of compassion.

The consciousness of an "Afraid man" cannot bloom. It is imprisoned by the fear of uncertainty. It is as if you have planted a banyan tree in a flower pot. The potential of that tree is not enough; a space is also required. The limitation of the flower pot gets imposed upon the tree and becomes the tree's limitation. The potential of our soul is also not enough; a space is required. The self created four walls have to be dropped consciously and the fear of uncertainty has to be exposed to the light of your awareness. Instead of becoming afraid because of your fears, you need to become aware of them. You need to look at the trembling of your soul from the dimension of absolute faith instead of trembling yourself. It will dissolve the trembling and reinforce the faith. Instead of jumping from here to there and from there to here at the sight of a snake, just stay where you are and you will be surprised by the outcome. Fear always jumps around; faith stays where it is.

Fear creates a trembling in your soul while faith provides it with stability. At the surface, the cause of our fear could be incidental and momentary but at the deepest level, the cause of all our fears is the subconscious knowing that our fate is at the mercy of a billion laws beyond our control. When we see events happening around us that do not synchronize with our own blueprint of life, the gap between the way things are and the way we wish them to be becomes our sense of powerlessness and out of that sense of powerlessness springs uncertainty. It is this uncertainty which makes us tremble and the only way to negate this trembling is to have a faith that is at least as big as the cause of our fear. Fear and despair are a darkness that can only be dispelled with faith and hope. Our life may be at the mercy of a billion laws but those billion laws come from the same one perfection. It is this perfection we need to have faith in; it is this perfection we need to trust.

Faith develops like a muscle of our body; you have to feed it properly and force it to grow. The practice with which you cultivate faith is - religious gambling. The gambler in the ordinary world puts money at stake in order to earn more of it. In religious gambling, you play with the faith you have got in order to earn more of the same. Unless you offer the reins of your life into the hands of the existence, you cannot develop a communion with it. You cannot overcome the fear of a king cobra by playing with a snake made up of rubber. You cannot overcome the fear of height by jumping from 10 feet. The odds must be high. Greater is the gamble; stronger will be the communion. Faith does not lie within the precincts of all that can be calculated with the mind. It lies beyond the calculations of the mind. Faith is not like the elastic band of a bungee jumper or the parachute of a sky diver; faith is that which takes care of all the variables which could go wrong and make you hit the ground. If you can calculate it, it is not faith. There has to be something for the existence to take care of. Our fear is because of the variables that are beyond our control; our faith is our communion with the one which controls all these variables.

The common man tries to secure everything against uncertainty. A nine to five government job, an arranged marriage, a house well built, a financial backup, social contacts, a religion to follow, a political party to belong to and so on. A Yogi throws away all of these and embraces uncertainty to go in pursuit of truth. This is faith. The Yogi has a lot of it right from the beginning. He is a born gambler; a man of faith. The common man lives in fear; the Yogi rarely trembles. Without faith, a Richard Alpert, professor of an Oxford University could not have dared to throw away a career as prestigious as his, left his home town and travelled all the way to the Himalayas, passing through countries as turbulent as Afghanistan and Pakistan. He had tons of it right from the beginning. Without faith, he could not have bloomed into Baba Ram Dass. He spent the prime of his incarnation in realizing the truth. Life lived in fear is like mathematics; life lived in faith is like poetry. No one can discover faith while clinging to security. You have to learn how to swim in the waters of uncertainty. You have to have the gambler's heart.

In clinging to security, we turn our back towards uncertainty and start avoiding and running away from things that threaten our comfort zone. But whatever we avoid and run away from becomes a source of our fear. In choosing this and avoiding that, we sow the seeds of fear. We try to pass the ocean of life through the pipe of our comfort zone and when we fail to do so, we feel threatened. Fear is born out of this knowing, deep down that we will never ever be able to secure everything from uncertainty, no matter how hard we try. The harder we try, the more we tremble. The more we try to escape from our vulnerability; the more vulnerable we feel. Life is not that simple and straight; everything is paradoxical and mysterious. Freedom from fear lies in accepting and embracing impermanence and this acceptance will come from your faith. So faith is the only antidote for fear. Where there is fear; bring faith.

When we decide to deal with our fear, we will have to deal with it at two levels; the conscious and the subconscious. The conscious fear is the fear stimulated by a real life situation in the present whereas the subconscious fear is the fear that has layered or accumulated in our being because of all the situations in the past which were similar to the one we are facing. Subconscious fear is the one that sponsors our nightmares. Since we are not facing any real life danger in a dream, the fear and the threats could only have come from some deep layering of our mind. The most efficient way to reach out to these layers is by meditating and witnessing. When you meditate, things start surfacing; when you witness them, they are dispelled. You have to stir your consciousness with real life gambling and then dissolve the fear that moves from the subconscious layer to the conscious one. I will try to explain it with a real life example. Suppose you are very possessive about your spouse and your soul is frequently trembling due to the fear of a betrayal. Now, the only way to liberate yourself from this trembling is to give all the freedom your spouse asks for, let him or her be totally responsible for his or her Karma, be only concerned about your own character and have faith in the one that is watching all of us all day - all night. There is no need for you to reduce your being to that of a watchman. You can liberate yourself from this fear and this self imprisonment the moment you decide to do so.

If you keep on consciously dispelling your fears and phobias with your awareness and faith, the subconscious layers of your being will soon run out of stock and your tranquility will expand into all the dimensions. The enlightened master Thich Nhat Hanh shares a great insight with all of us when he says, "As long as fear is there, our happiness cannot be perfect". All phobias must be eliminated from our being in order to create space for a happiness that doesn't tremble. As long as fear is there, you will even be afraid of happiness because subconsciously you will be aware that when happiness walks out of your life, sadness walks in. You will see happiness not as happiness but as an invitation to sadness. So you will be sad when you are sad and afraid when you are happy. We are not only afraid of dying, we are also afraid of living. Through the incarnations, we have become familiar with the temperament of life; its' unexpected twists and turns, its' surprising and sometimes shocking challenges. Unless we grow beyond the reach of misery at the ordinary level of existence we cannot get rid of the basic fear that runs through our days and nights like the thread that runs through the beads of a Mala.

Now, what happens to the fear of those who love to live on the edge? People like the dacoit, the car-racer, the gangster, the drug lord and the terrorist? Are they able to conquer fear and live the life that lies beyond it? Well, one thing is certain that these people are more in contact with their faith than an ordinary man. The variables of risk involved in their way of living are so many that the only constant that keeps them going is their faith. But their faith is not in harmony with the compassion of the existence. It does not synchronize with the universal desire. Life was not given to us to be carelessly tossed around. The purpose of our incarnation is not to play hide and seek with death and especially not in a manner in which the lives of fellow beings are at stake. Though they are able to step out of the perimeter of fear, the growth of people living on the edge is so one-dimensional that they are not able to stay there for very long. In most of the cases, they don't even have an awareness to taste their fearlessness. Their life is like an orgasm; intense but short lived. I think there is no point in killing yourself just to know the taste of death; there is no point in throwing away your precious incarnation just to know the taste of fearlessness. The method should be such that it can be taught to someone who has worldly duties to perform and whose life is more meaningful than his death. And that is exactly what we are here to explore.

The challenges of ordinary life are enough for your spiritual growth; there is no need for you to go in search of extremes. There are already enough extremes hidden behind the veil of our incarnation. Isn't it an extreme that we will all have to see our parents age and die? Isn't it an extreme that we will be separated from all our near and dear ones sooner or later according to the unfolding of our incarnation? Isn't it an extreme that in spite of all that we know, we will have to helplessly watch our closed ones refuse to listen, make mistakes and suffer? Isn't it an extreme that no matter how good we are, we will still be treated badly by those who cannot see what we can? Isn't it an extreme that we will be betrayed by those that we have loved, wounded by those that we have healed, attacked by those that we have protected and insulted by those that we have pulled out of dungeons? Isn't it an extreme that we will be violently opposed for speaking the truth, despised for not learning the cunning ways of the world and hated for reminding others, with our own character, the lack of strength in them? Life is already hard enough; you don't have to make it more painful by volunteering for an extreme.

It has taken incarnations for your fear to develop; it will take a few years to dispel it. Don't worry. With practice, persistence and patience, you will be able to do that. First of all become aware of the fact that a great percentage of your fears are pure imagination; there is no real situation to be dealt with. But if you keep on entertaining them in your mind and keep on feeding them with the energy of thoughts, they could start materializing. The real fear is not the fear itself; it is the power of the mind to convert an imagination into reality. Now, this could become your latest fear. So just develop faith and use your mind as a friend not a foe. Dispel your negativity with faith and create something beautiful with your mind.

Some fears are no doubt genuine. They should be handled wisely. If your health has been deteriorating continuously over the past few years, then the resultant fear of conditions worsening is not something to be taken lightly. Faith of course is essential but some action will also be required to produce positive results. In situations like these, the purpose of fear is to wake you up like an alarm clock. You must not go back to sleep. Dispel the fear with faith but also do something about the real life situation that is sponsoring it. Faith is not a substitute for Karma. They both have their own significance and their own role to play in the unfolding of our incarnation. If you have not earned a single penny in the last ten years, have got married and are about to become a parent, then the fear of poverty is genuine. It is not an imagination and is not irrational. You will have to have faith but you will also have to earn a decent living and learn how to survive in this world. Every fear is not a sickness and something to be cured; a few of them are an expression of God's concern for you. You have to be wise enough to distinguish between the real ones and the virtual ones and then deal with them accordingly.

Some fear can also be eliminated from your being by consciously going into the past and standing in the thickness of events that instilled it into you. You may have never given it a thought that we all deliberately avoid looking back at such events. But in doing so, we allow that instilled fear to remain in our being like an unhealed wound. Every such fear is a wound and has to be gently healed with the energy of faith and compassion. You cannot change your past but you can change what it means to you. The events that sowed fear in you were all opportunities for you to overcome fear and develop faith. If you had gone through these events fearlessly, you would have risen above fear and above the challenges of day to day life. Your character would have bloomed like a lotus and you would have come to know the taste of unwavering faith long ago.

There are fears that can totally go unnoticed. Two of such fears are the fear of intimacy and the fear of success. The fear of intimacy needs to be healed in order to weave a beautiful world of relationships and the fear of success must be overcome to invite abundance into your life. Every time someone lets you down, the fragile bond of affection that exists between you and mankind is wounded. If you keep on piling up these wounds inside your being, they can go into the making of a very fundamental regret that can hold you back from entering into any intimate relationship. The wounds must be healed and they must not be allowed to pile up.

Wisdom can heal all such wounds. Wisdom makes it easy for you to accept and embrace the fact that people are exactly what God has made them and if they have disappointed you, then your expectations from them must have been more than what they could live up to. When this knowing ripens, it takes the form of compassion and when you look at people while being firmly rooted in compassion yourself, you don't only see what they do to you, you can also see what they are doing to themselves by sowing the seeds of suffering with their Karma. Wisdom does not let you get stuck in behaviors, shortcomings, weaknesses, inclinations and tendencies. You can take an aerial view of all these details of life and see from above, the pattern they make. You come to realize what a Saint meant when he said, "In my world, nothing goes wrong".

We are afraid of an intimacy because it requires the opening up of our heart, exposing our being to the other, creating space for the other and volunteering for the probability of a letdown. Investing trust in a relationship is like investing money in a piece of real estate; both demand a lot of investigation if you don't wish to incur a loss. It is easy to forget a financial loss; it is far more difficult to forget a betrayal. Emotions are really a very sophisticated stuff and great care is needed in their handling. A trust earned in twenty years can be shattered in 20 seconds and once someone has let you down, you may be unable to allow him or her into your heart with the same love and generosity. This fear can be cured by creating space in you for the "Humanness" of a human-being. You must not expect the behavior of a Christ from a common man. An ordinary man will behave like an ordinary man. Allow that behavior to be the way it is and do not resist it. The people who have failed to live up to your expectations could be your job. They may have come in contact with you because they needed you more than you needed them. It was not an accident; it was all according to the unfolding of the divine will.

Every enlightened being has his own method of filtering souls in order to protect his compassion. This is very important. The heart of an enlightened one is like a garden of roses; you cannot let stray animals to just walk in and ruin everything. It has to be protected from intrusions and invasions. What we call an Ashram is simply a filtering of the souls and if carried out efficiently, the process can create a soil where intimate relationships can be grown. The best remedy for emotional wounds is a few meaningful relationships; your relationship with your master or the existence, being at the top of the list. These relationships can heal your fear of intimacy and assist you in restoring your heart to its normal compassionate self. As far as the world outside the Ashram is concerned, the dance of forms should be embraced as it is and the heart kept open to it all. But a safe distance between you and the world may have to be maintained without being uncompassionate. To the ordinary eye, it may all appear very paradoxical. People may also call you weird. But that is the only way for these two planes of reality to co-exist, the Sansaar (World) and Nirvaan (Enlightenment).

Intimacy means becoming one with the other and ego exists in duality and conflict. Therefore, ego has a great role to play in aggravating the fear of intimacy. Intimacy requires a mutual unwritten contract between two souls to offer their individualities in the service of a common cause. The ego is not interested in all this. It wants to protect and defend its uniqueness in order to stand out. So when two ascetics experience the fear of intimacy in coming close to each other, it is most probably due to their egos since the chances of a let-down are very little in such cases. But unless a good man overcomes this fear, his goodness cannot be of a very great value to the rest of the world. For the blessings of the virtuous to be showered upon the rest of the world, their virtues must be offered in the service of a cause that is bigger than their individual differences. The molecules of H2o must come together to make a water that can quench the thirst of the masses.

Another fear that can easily go unnoticed is the fear of success. We all want to succeed but we are all afraid of success. When we are miserable, defeated, sick and unhappy, we feel at home. When we are blissful, triumphant, healthy and happy, we feel as if we have come away from home and long to go back. We have lived in misery for so long that it has become our residence. We are comfortable with a bit of happiness every now and then but we cannot stay in a state of bliss. We consciously try to eliminate suffering from our life but subconsciously keep on creating suffering for ourselves in order to remain in touch with it. Success, joy, peace and oneness are an alien way of living for us. They all feel strange to us, sometimes even uncomfortable. All our self-defeating habits are a way of avoiding success. With success comes limelight and with limelight come jealousy, envy, criticism, hatred and enmity. All these things force us out of our comfort zone. So we unintentionally try to avoid the whole package.

We are more interested in the journeys than the destinations because once we reach there, we can either stay there or go back i.e. return; the romance of travel has been squeezed out of the whole thing. People spend days in climbing up to a temple situated at a high altitude, stay there for half an hour and then begin the return journey. The lack of oxygen and the minus temperatures force them to go back. The first feeling that comes to you when you reach a destination is the feeling that you have been robbed of the romance of the journey. Success, bliss, peace and enlightenment are all destinations and we all are, on a very deeper level, afraid of them because once we reach there, there will be nowhere to go. So we try to prolong our endeavors and postpone our reaching in sophisticated and paradoxical ways. On one hand, we try to succeed but on the other, we avoid success. We meditate for hours every day but we are afraid of enlightenment. This basic contradiction in our desire system can create a lot of confusion in our life. The fear of success is one of these basic contradictions in our being.

In general, whatever makes you tremble is a fear and needs to be replaced with faith. But there is something that needs to be understood. This trembling has nothing to do with cowardice. It is simply a spiritual ailment which needs to be cured. Everyone is trembling but everyone is not aware of it. The ascetic becomes aware of his fears; his trembling. This awareness first of all defines the fear i.e. provides it with a shape and a size. Then, with conscious effort, the fear can be dispelled. Awareness works like naturopathy or Reiki; in the first part of the cure, the ailment is made noticeable and brought to the surface of our being. In the second part, it is healed with compassion and faith. With spiritual practices, things do not just vaporize; they are first brought from the subconscious into the conscious and then treated accordingly. Whether it is lust or anger, whether it is greed, attachment or fear, the method is the same; the fog of it that is scattered all over your being is condensed into a more tangible form so that it becomes easy for your awareness to do something about it. At one stage in its elimination, your fear will become very thick and your trembling very noticeable. Don't be disheartened; it's just a process. Allow it to flow towards its completion and help it to mature.

When you allow your fear to ripen, it automatically falls off your soul and you discover a new kind of living;"Fearless Living." It is a living that does not belong to this world. The fear of a physical death and the fear of the death of the ego rule this world like a dictator. The mortality of the body and the vulnerability of the ego are the breeding grounds of almost all our fears. But when someone manages to find his immortal self and does not identify with the body or the ego any more, the very foundation of fear has been destroyed. The radiance of a fearless man is like that of a full moon;

the blooming is so complete. The energy that was blocked due to fear starts flowing like a river. By including both the death of the body and the death of the ego in his consciousness, he has expanded into a space unknown to the masses. Fearlessness is not just an attitude; it is a dimension and it can be so liberating that there are a few who refuse to go back to the world living in fear e.g. the Martyrs.

Now fearless does not mean reckless. The Saint is always fearless but never reckless. He has great respect for his own life and the life of all other living beings. He may jump into danger if the situation asks for that but he will never do it just to prove something to himself or to others. All our Martyrs were Saints. They had realized that the fear of the masses was being exploited by the rulers and to free the nation, they had to first free themselves of all the possible comfort zones, all the fears. The world living in fear looks at a Martyr from a different angle. The fearless Martyr looks at this world from a different space. The world looks at the life of a Martyr in terms of death, pain, sacrifice and suffering; the Martyr looks at his own life in terms of immortality, compassion, giving, expansion and liberty.

But if we are reckless, we can create a situation like Afghanistan. It is a country where people die first and live later. Death is accepted as a part of life on a mass level and the average life expectancy is 43 years. Afghanis cannot live without battle. Their fighting instincts have been developed to such an extent that they have to have a war every now and then just to feel alive. From 1979 to 1989 they were fighting against the Soviets. Then for almost a decade they were fighting amongst each other. After that it was the Americans. They have to fight. They have to live the life that exists beyond the fear of death. It is in their blood. But to enjoy the taste of that life they have to throw away all the subtleness of a human incarnation. It is the price they pay for the life they choose. Their life revolves around opium, bullets, automatic weapons, battles and wars. There is no space in it for peace, music, dance, education and all the softer colors of life. So if you are born in Afghanistan, the best choice for you would be to love being a warrior and when you are a warrior, the bullets become your beads, the automatic weapon is your holy book and the battlefield is your meditation hall. But this is not the only way to live without fear.

There is no need to jump into a battle and kill each other just to live beyond fear. Dying to the body and dying to the ego is enough. Life in itself is a battle and there are challenges enough to prove your might. You don't have to throw your whole family, community, state or nation into the fire of conflict and war just to get your valor certified. You can be fearless and non-violent. You can be fearless and compassionate. You can be fearless and peaceful. To dispel fear, you need faith but to cultivate faith you don't need a battlefield. A battlefield just happens to be one of the situations in which man is in a very deep communion with God. There is almost a situation every day where that communion can be established and the dimension of faith can be tapped. Our soul trembles once or twice everyday; that trembling can be a path to faith if used wisely.

The energy of faith is triggered by a deep and pure surrender. You cannot fake a faith. The surrender has to be deep and it has to be pure. It has to come from the core of your being, the heart of your being. When someone jumps from a helicopter, almost a kilometer from the ground, with nothing but a parachute to ensure a safe landing, the surrender is deep and pure. The person has offered his destiny in the hands of God. The person could even be someone who does not believe in God. But if it is so, he cannot believe in the parachute either. God does not depend upon our beliefs. When we drop our defenses, God reveals itself. When you are in the mid of the air, falling down like a stone, science is not enough to guarantee a safe landing. Faith develops in situations like these and the nature of life is such that we are always in the mid of the air, away from the ground, away from the helicopter; hence the trembling, hence the fear. Faith is therefore as essential as the health of our body and mind. We can say that our faith decides the health of our soul; our spiritual health. Just as we need exercise for a healthy body and meditation for a healthy mind, we need faith for a healthy soul.

There is no doubt a lot of faith in Afghanistan. Wherever there is fearless living; there will be faith. When someone jumps out of his comfort zone, he enters the zone of faith. Saying good bye to the luxuries of ordinary living is not that easy. The country may have earned a bad name because of Islamic Fundamentalism but there are a great percentage of sincere peasants who just wish to live with dignity and die with honor. No other country has witnessed that much of warfare and no other country has lived on the edge for that long. Afghanistan is the most significant experiment of God on life that exists beyond the comfort zone of a 21st century man. The kids can be seen playing their innocent games in empty abandoned tanks and 15 year olds are carrying machine guns and rocket launchers. The fighters are so used to living fearlessly that they are not even discouraged by the price they pay for that kind of a life in terms of widows, orphans, child and women casualties, homelessness and poverty. The dark side of such a life includes much more than that. It is a price that most of us would not like to pay. We want faith but not at the cost of peace and it's possible. It is possible to live fearlessly but peacefully.

Every warrior, at some point in his life, is able to see the oneness behind the separation. The word enemy and all the bitterness, hatred and revenge that goes with it, sooner or later fades out and a fighter wakes up to the dance of life; the truth hidden behind the fog of all the melodrama. When the divine will reveals itself to the warrior, from an ordinary soldier, he is evolved into God's warrior. He has included the enemy and expanded. He has grown beyond victories and defeats. He can see through the celebration of a victory and the mourning of a defeat. He can observe the perfect laws of life hidden behind the chaos of the battlefield and he can listen to the silence behind all the noise. All fear is dissolved; all trembling is gone. The understanding of the bigger picture takes care of all the minor threats and the consciousness is elevated to a higher plane of reality. The anger is replaced by compassion and the duality is replaced by the wisdom of oneness. It's the warrior's way of getting enlightened. It's Arjun's way of becoming available to a higher perspective.

The ascetic has his own way of expressing his fearlessness. There's a real story of an enlightened Rishi (Monk) who lived in a cave by the side of a jungle, somewhere in the mountains. There were all kinds of wild animals in the jungle. One evening, when the Rishi was meditating outside his cave, a lion happened to pay him a visit. The Rishi showed absolutely no signs of fear, opened his eyes slowly, got up from his squatting position and outstretched his arms in the gesture of an embrace, as if to greet the guest that had appeared from nowhere. The lion, as if hypnotized by the compassion of the monk, fell into his arms, behaved like a pet, cuddled him for minutes and then peacefully sat outside the cave all night. That is the power of faith. That is the kind of life that unfolds itself in the absence of fear. There is a whole different world that exists beyond fear, in the realm of love and compassion.

There is another story of an enlightened being who happened to be a Muslim. In the moments of ecstasy, he used to repeat the words, "I am God' and this was something totally unacceptable to the people he was living amongst. According to the local customs, anyone who claimed to be the almighty was to be publically executed. So the Fakeer (Saint), when brought before the local council agreed to the decision that the next time he claims to be God, he should be beheaded there and then. That moment arrived soon and in his ecstatic state he started shouting, "I am Brahma (God)", "I am Brahma". The one who was supposed to execute him unsheathed his sword, raised it before carrying out the orders and then struck with the speed of lightening so that he did not have to do it twice. But to the utter amazement of everyone present, the sword went through the neck of the Fakeer without harming even a single hair on his skin. It happened so three times and forced the locals to give up. When he came back to his senses, the Fakeer wanted to know what had happened. They told him as it is. "Then it must be God only" he said. Beyond fear, all this is possible.

The Bible also says that if you have faith as much as a mustard seed and you tell a mountain to move, it shall move. Such faith can exist only where there is no fear. The nature of the energy of fear is such that you cannot expect miracles from it. The flowers of miracles bloom on the soil of faith. You cannot expect seeds thrown on a marbled floor to grow into beautiful flowers. The power contained by a faith as much as a mustard seed is like the power contained by a nuclear bomb. What matters is not the size of the container but the stuff inside. A potato cannot be compared to a grenade of the same size. The difference between fear and faith is not quantitative but qualitative. Living in fear is like living on earth whereas living in faith is like living in the space beyond gravity. You come in contact with laws you had never tasted before. The world of men and women living in faith is a world completely different from the world of men and women living in fear.

Like anger, lust, greed attachment and ego, fear keeps you belonging to the world which Lao Tse calls, "The world of ten thousand things". When we get attached to all that we have got, we are afraid of losing it in some way or the other. Now, all that we have got belongs to this world and therefore clinging to it will keep us clinging to this world. We tremble because we are subconsciously aware of the impermanence of things and we are afraid of the fundamentals of life that discourage attachment and clinging. Our trembling is because of trying to run away from the inevitable. We can see impermanence approaching us from all directions. Our relationships are changing, our neighborhood is changing, our body is changing and so is our mind and soul. People are dying, relationships are dying, hopes are dying, desires are dying, commitments are dying and loyalties are dying. We tremble because we can hear the footsteps of impermanence approaching us. We tremble because we are unable to embrace it.

Why do you think we are afraid of the enlightened? We are afraid because in their presence, we can hear the footsteps of impermanence even louder. Their wisdom amplifies the sound. In the light of their detachment, we can see through our own clinging and the very foundations of our ideology are shaken. More than 90% of the people avoid the enlightened with clever excuses. A lot of them even change their path if they see such a man walking in their direction in a street. It is the fear of an illusion being shattered. The false is always afraid of the truth. The clever is afraid of the pious. The thief is afraid of the sentry. In the eyes of the enlightened, we see a sentry standing at the gate of a soul. We know that we cannot steal and escape with our arguments. Our mind finds itself trapped in its own justifications. We are also afraid of the enlightened because there is no one better equipped to kill our ego. Our enemies can only kill our body but a Saint can kill our ego and he can do that without a weapon. He can do it with love, compassion and forgiveness. Our ego fears a defeat more than anything else and it can see that in confronting a Saint a defeat is absolutely certified; hence the trembling. The fear of the enlightened is one of the most unacknowledged fears and needs to be dispelled in order to allow the soul to come in contact with those who can make it evolve and help it expand.

Like every other fear, the fear of the man who knows, is an opportunity for you to develop faith and that faith is in the very presence of this man. He has lived the divine will and can provide you with an assurance that it is absolutely safe to "Let go and let God." Shri Ram Dass has been a lot with dying people in their last moments and has helped them in migrating from this world to that. Rarely someone goes that far and when someone does, he should be listened to. He says, "My experience has been that it is perfectly safe to die." It's a great assurance. The man of faith is a source of the assurance that it is perfectly safe to live in faith. He has allowed the flow of his life to be decided by the divine will and has checked the interference of his fears in his relationship with the ultimate. The very presence of this man can dispel your insecurities. The world lives in fear and therefore fuels your trembling; this man lives in faith and therefore inspires you to step out of fear. He is not something to be avoided; he is something to be sought because he can cure your trembling and bless you with stability.

Our trembling is sponsored by sources that we may have never even given a thought. One of them is, guilt associated with the awareness of our own actions in the past. When we evolve spiritually, we become aware of the law of Karma; the precision with which it operates. We also wake up to the negativity and violence in our own past Karma. Subconsciously, we are busy a lot of the time, preparing ourselves for God's punishment. Though we are unable to forgive others, we would surely like to be forgiven. The word "Sin" triggers our trembling. We become afraid of our own Karma. We start seeking a refuge and we find it in the unconditional love of a Saint. The Saint introduces us to the flip side of the law of Karma- the law of forgiveness. In his presence, we learn that in order to be forgiven, you have to forgive. If we are harsh with others; the existence is going to be harsh with us. If we are kind to others, the existence is going to be kind to us. It is one way of interpreting "Give and you shall receive".

Forgiveness not only heals the trembling due to guilt; it also takes care of fear due to anticipation. A lot of our anxiety is because of anticipation. We fear that he or she may do this or that to us. We fear this or that may happen to us or someone we love. Fear due to anticipation is fear sponsored by the future and it is because of being unable to open ourselves to the future, to accept and embrace it. Forgiveness starts with accepting the past, then includes the present and gradually expands into the future. Forgiveness dissolves the barrier due to our resistance to the divine will. It blesses us with the insight, "Whatever happens, happens for the good". This insight adds strength to our faith and we are able to see the wellbeing hidden behind the painful details of a human incarnation. It assists us in pulling ourselves out of the density of a misery and becoming available to the whispers of God.

When you step out of fear, embrace your vulnerability and open up to the divine will, your consciousness starts expanding into dimensions that you had never known before. You discover that there is a complete world that exists beyond the obvious which we are all born into. You feel as if the songs were always there in the ethers but since you did not have a transistor that could tune in to those frequencies, you could never listen to them. I would call this world, "The world of compassion" or "The world of faith". It is so different from the ordinary world that the man who lives in it does not belong to the ordinary world any more. The priorities undergo such a huge change that it becomes difficult to find a common interest between a man of faith and a man of the ordinary world. Ascetics have often called it, "The jaggery of the dumb". Just as a dumb man cannot explain the taste of jaggery to those who can speak, the man of faith cannot explain the taste of faith to those who are living in fear. He is rendered speechless by the mystery that surrounds his experience.

We all touch the world of faith every now and then but are unable to stay there because of the gravity of lust, anger, attachment, greed and ego. We all know the taste of love, characterized by a deep fulfillment and an absence of desires. But dwelling in faith or love is not the same thing as a fleeting glance at it. To dwell in faith, you have to uproot your soul from the ordinary world. If you are trying to strike a balance between these two worlds, you are basically living on the cusp and the cusp is not the same thing as the world beyond it. Like ice, hot water and steam, the ordinary world, the transition phase and the world of faith, though all, the creator's creation, are fundamentally poles apart. There is no way you can compare Mr. Bill gates with Shri Hanuman Ji. And if by chance they happen to stand at the same spot on earth it would be like a man from earth standing next to a man from Mars. Men of faith have been often crucified by the ordinary folks because their presence, their being, is a threat to the ideology of the mass. It is easy to crucify one than to transform a billion. All these crucifixions point towards the communication gap between the man of fear and the man of faith or in other words, the man of ego and the man of love.

The deeper you move into the world of faith, the closer you come to all those laws of the existence that were not accessible to you because of your doubt. One of these laws is the law of manifestation. What a man of doubt manifests with years of thinking, a man of faith can manifest with a single thought. Fear makes us crawl on the ground; faith makes us fly. That which is nothing less than a miracle for a man of fear and doubt, is routine for a man of faith. But it becomes hard to explain, just the way the experience of an astronaut is hard to feel for someone who has lived on the surface of the earth for incarnations. We have gotten used to living in fear and doubt just the way we have gotten used to gravity. In the beginning, faith feels as alien to the soul as the absence of a gravitational pull to the body. But after some time, you get accustomed to it and are able to welcome the expansion of the consciousness. The power of faith is like nuclear power; it cannot be comprehended by someone who is used to weighing things in kilograms.

The secret of religiousness is in allowing fear to introduce you to faith. When a situation in life gives birth to fear, don't panic. Stand still, withdraw all your senses from the external variables, root yourself in your endurance and allow the energy of fear to become an invitation for faith. No wind is strong enough to last forever. Things come and go. Every situation in our life unfolds according to a million laws and the best way to handle them is by being still. We must not create new stuff because of the old one. In this standing still you will cultivate faith. You will be able to experience and know the forces that take care of you when you trust them. You will discover that faith is not some accidental thing; it unfolds according to an exact discipline and the most basic condition for this unfolding is the allowing of fear to mature by not entertaining it.

Fear is the weight of this world; faith is the taste of God. We need to understand that existence does not know us by our name, gender, religion, nationality or social status; it knows us as a packet of energy. It knows us as the kind of energy we are and the kind of vibrations we send into the cosmos. A man living in fear sends out vibrations of doubt and suspicion and produces results that synchronize with his frequency, thus certifying his fear and providing him with a reason to be afraid. It's a vicious cycle and guaranteed to keep you in fear. The existence responds to your vibrations like an echo. On the other hand, a man of faith emanates trust and acceptance from his being and the existence responds to it by living up to his expectations. The existence provides him with a parental care and thus encourages him to trust and accept. Both these men are connected to the existence but the man living in fear is unable to know and understand the divine ways because of his own reluctance to jump out of the comfort zone. From fear to faith is a big quantum leap but sooner or later it is us who have to make it. The existence cannot do it for us. It can only encourage our initiative.

We are all God's children; God's babies. When we live in fear, we are like a baby that cries all the time. Anyone who has brought up kids knows what it is to bring up a baby that gets up in the morning with a cry and goes to bed crying at night. It is a bit annoying and takes away some of the beauty and fun from the relationship between you and your child. The beauty of our relationship with the cosmos also depends upon whether we live in faith or fear. It is the most significant of all our relationships and our destiny is going to unfold according to it. We ought to make it as harmonious as possible and one of the ways to do that is to invite faith wherever there is fear, to invite light wherever there is darkness. There is no point in cutting yourself off from the infinity of Brahma by constructing walls of doubt around your being. There is no point in converting the whole existence into a threat with your fear when it is possible to befriend the universe and allow it to assist you in realizing your dreams and realizing your true potential.

Chapter 8 - GREED

All greed is basically the human attempt to fill the emptiness that is due to lack of love. Our soul is like a vessel and it is gratified only when it is full of love. But when we try to stuff it with things other than love, we cultivate the habit of consumption. The more we consume, the emptier we feel because every consumption is a taking and love is a giving. We are like a depressed person who is overeating in order to derive some happiness from food. The fundamental error goes unnoticed and the error is that pleasures of the senses cannot be a substitute for love. Our greed is due to this fundamental error.

But what makes it possible for love to quench the soul? Though love is one of those mysteries that are beyond all explanations, I will try my best to get as close to it as I can. The dimension of love is the one that synchronizes the most with the core nature of existence. When someone falls into the dimension of love he or she falls into the existence. The separation is dissolved and the whole universe belongs to the soul. When it is all yours, there is nothing to run after, nothing to hoard and nothing to consume. We own, possess, hoard and consume because of the separation, because of the duality. Love first converts you into a vacuum and then fills it with the existence. When a bucket of water is poured into a glass, it not only feels quenched, it overflows. The day your soul becomes available to the dimension of love, there is an overflow of joy and greed is something of the past.

The emptiness within is the root of all desires. Someone is busy stuffing it with foods and drinks. Someone is busy stuffing it with stimulants, intoxicants and tranquilizers. Someone is busy stuffing it with sex and all the pleasures of the senses. Someone is busy stuffing it with extravagance and flirting. Someone is busy stuffing it with money, real estate, automobiles and luxuries. Someone is busy stuffing it with fame and power. Someone is busy stuffing it with degrees and diplomas. Someone is busy stuffing it with spiritual powers and higher knowledge. But the emptiness remains and the lack of something beyond our understanding still dominates our being. It is this emptiness that gives birth to all the spiritual practices because spiritual practices are nothing but an effort to understand this lack and then do something about it instead of wasting an incarnation playing hide and seek with it.

Imagine having in your house a well that has got no bottom. Now imagine trying to fill it with money, power, fame, sex and all that you can possibly desire. We all have in us a well with no bottom - the well of greed; the well of incessant wanting. Without meditation, without a spiritual practice, there is nothing that can provide this well with a bottom and that is what makes meditation essential for a fulfillment. Indulgence in the pleasures of the senses cannot fill the well of greed. It only leads to addictions of all kinds and addiction has been defined by Dr. Wayne Dyer as, "Never having enough of what you don't want". If we don't do something about our greed we fall prey to our endless wanting and get caught up in a very helpless and hopeless kind of situation. Our being is reduced to a hunger that can never be satisfied and our desires keep on torturing us all the time. Our own mind becomes a constant torment to us.

A child gets love from everyone and is therefore not greedy. The constant bathing in the vibrations of love fulfils the soul of the child. But as the child grows and starts moving around freely, all those "loves" become "possessions" and "dominations." This is when the seeds of greed are sown. The lack of unconditional love in the life of an adult becomes the breeding ground for wants and desires of all sorts. The love starved society educates all of us in greed. Does anyone teach us to give? No. Does anyone teach us to forgive? No. Does anyone educate us in compassion? No. Does anyone teach us to sit silently for an hour and meditate? No. We learn all this on our own when we go through the agonies of our incarnation. Our whole education system is based upon cut throat competition and survival of the fittest. There is no space in it for the development of the greatest human virtues which are freely available – love and compassion.

Two of the greatest components of what we call the world or the society are the home and the market-place. Now, the market-place thrives on fanning our desires, our greed. Continuous bombardment of advertising, forces us into wanting things that we could easily live without. As long as we are rooted in this world and our consciousness totally belongs to it, we are destined to live a life driven by greed. It is only when we succeed in pulling ourselves out of this ocean of mass consciousness that the hold of greed upon our soul loosens. Till then, even our own self is not available to us; it is a puppet in the hands of forces outside us. We keep on dancing to the tunes of this world and call it survival, livelihood or struggle for success without recognizing the spiritual slavery underneath the obvious. If attachment is what binds us to our family, then greed is what binds us to the rest of the world.

When you look at this world with eyes full of greed, it looks like a hell; when you look at it with eyes full of love, it looks like a heaven. Greed makes it a hell because it converts your life into an ocean of unfulfilled desires. Love makes the same world a heaven because you have no expectations from it and where there are no expectations, there can be no disappointment. When there are no desires to be fulfilled; only love to be shared, the whole situation becomes very promising. When you look at the world with greed in your eyes, you see people richer than you, more powerful than you, more famous than you. But when you look at the world with love in your eyes, you only see a love starved mankind. The layer of greed makes it impossible for you to see the marvel that life is. The materialistic wants make you deaf to the sounds of God, numb to the taste of the divine and blind to the mystery hidden behind the veil of physical forms.

Greed thinks in terms of magnitude and quantity. It thinks that by gathering 100 small satisfactions, it can create a big fulfillment out of them. This is a big mistake that every materialist makes. Though alcohol can be made from sweet potato but by eating 100 sweet potatoes you are not going to get intoxicated. The process of making alcohol cannot be bypassed. Similarly, life has to be processed in order to know the taste of real fulfillment and there is only one kind of it – love. Love does not have any types and subtypes. If you have not reached it yet, you cannot be fulfilled. The soul knows the taste of its source and therefore cannot be deceived. But it is not something that you can cultivate while indulging in one thousand different pleasures of the senses. Indulgence is simply not the process with which you can create love. Indulgence is the path of greed. The path of love is – giving and forgiving.

Greed works on the principle, "The more I have; the happier I am going to be." With this principle as the backbone of every thought, when we look at the world, we see those who have got more than us. We see those who have got stuff a hundred times, a thousand times or even a million times more than us and we get depressed. Greed is a guaranteed formula for a 24 hour miserable life. It does not even let you sleep properly. It reminds you that while you are sleeping, there are those who are working and therefore getting ahead of you. As long as it is there, you will never have enough. Every time you try to pause for a while in order to rest and rejuvenate, it will make you run for more, if not physically then mentally. The momentum of the world will force its way into your being and you will be drifted along its currents like a leaf being drifted by an ocean. You will never be fulfilled, you will never be contented.

If you observe carefully, you will find that there is absolutely no fragrance in the life of the greedy. Their life is like the well which does not let anyone draw water from it – it stinks. The soul expands by giving and shrinks by taking. The one who has forgotten to give has forgotten to expand. Greed makes you incapable of giving and thus renders you poor on the most significant plane of existence. Greed wants more and when you want more how can you give what you have already got? It will be contradictory. Love, on the other hand, is like the well which supplies water to the whole village. The act of giving keeps it connected to the source and its pores healthy. Love connects us to our source by attuning us to that which holds all of the existence together and the relationship of man with the existence is a marriage of the highest order. It is the peak of all relationships. There is no pain of separation and the union is eternal.

We allow our incarnation to be driven along by the strong winds of greed because we never take the time to observe how long a satisfaction lasts. The taste of a food is felt by the tongue only. The "High" of every drug that alters your consciousness is followed by a "Low". No matter how much you sleep, when you wake up, you wake up to the same world and an orgasm of a sexual dance lasts only for a few seconds. All satisfactions are like an orgasm; you have not even had enough of them and they die. They are all momentary. If you look closely into the life of an ordinary man, he is basically repeating the same ten to fifteen satisfactions one after the other. These keep him going. You buy a new car and by the time you take it to the service station for the first paid service, the happiness has faded out. And you waited for years to buy this car. The deceiving nature of "Maya" is so apparent to eyes baptized by the Truth. But to the ordinary pair of eyes, everything in the world appears to be a potential satisfaction. Eyes clouded by greed cannot see the impermanence that is there in every atom of the existence and try to hold on to the fleeting pleasures.

As long as your being has not purified into love, your greed will only keep on changing forms. From material, it will become intellectual and from intellectual it will become spiritual. The material greed is busy gathering pleasures, the intellectual greed is busy gathering knowledge and titles and the spiritual greed is busy gathering spiritual powers and worshippers or followers. None of these games being played is love. It is only that your consumption has become subtle and sophisticated. Whether you eat a burger, a P.H.D or a miracle, as long as you are stuffing yourself with something from the outside, you are basically feeding your greed. Love does not feed itself; it feeds the other and gets fed in the process. The other is more significant. This is the basis on which to distinguish between greed and love. In greed, you are more significant than the other; in love the other is more significant than you.

Now, what we need to grasp is that without purifying our soul and inviting love into our being, we cannot get rid of our need to consume things for a satisfaction. We cannot fool our soul. The soul will lose interest in momentary pleasures only when it has started getting a regular and constant supply of bliss by dwelling in love. Simply throwing away all the pleasures will only make you bitter and lifeless. Renunciation cannot be faked. Indulgences fall away by themselves when the soul has got a better option. The soul never gives up "This" unless it is given "That" and that has to be better than this. It follows a very simple and straight logic. The greedy is greedy because he has not yet found love. Give him love and he will give up greed. And if you can't do that, there is no way you can convince him out of his hungers. He may take some time to respond to the mystery of compassion but it will ultimately seep into his soul. Love is the greatest power in this existence.

Love is the greatest blessing on earth but you have to be pure enough to invite it into your heart. You can start with giving and forgiving. These two are the spiritual practices that will gradually grow into compassion. You don't have to be very rich to give and forgive because these are attitudes, not something that is dependent upon your economic status. You can give someone a smile, a glass of water, a cup of tea, an idea, guidance or a few words of consolation. It will cost you absolutely nothing but will prepare your soul to forgive. Forgiving is not that easy for those who are not enlightened. Sometimes, the pain in forgiving is as much as in the injury concerned or even more than that. But without learning to forgive, you cannot invite love into your being. Forgiveness is the price you pay for deserving love. I have described the whole process to bring to your notice that the cultivation of compassion is an exact polar opposite of the cultivation of greed. When you don't grow a crop in a field, weeds automatically grow up. So when you do not cultivate compassion, greed automatically gets cultivated in your heart. When you don't teach your kids to give and forgive, they automatically learn to consume and hoard.

If you ask someone who is busy buying one acre of land after the other, "How many acres will be enough to gratify you?" he won't be able to tell how many. If you ask a womanizer how many women would be enough for his lust, he also won't be able to figure it out. The tragedy of mankind is that we sleep through our incarnations. We eat half a dozen times every day without ever trying to see what a hunger is. We sleep every night without ever trying to know what sleep is. Our wisdom of sex is slightly more than that of an animal and our satisfactions are almost the same as that of a fifteen year old. We never dare to question the norms of the society and we don't have the strength to believe in our heart. The world keeps on pushing us from behind and we keep on moving ahead aimlessly. Greed is basically a giant pattern of the mind being repeated day after day, month after month, year after year. It is so common because love is so rare; because love is a secret that this existence shares only with the elite. You cannot blame the world for being greedy; you can only pray to be blessed with love.

Greed is learnt by us as children and then imposed upon us by the world. Children are very acute observers. They are watching their parents all the time and learning from them. The parents, totally unaware of this, pass on their sicknesses to the next generation. Greed is one of these ailments that have been travelling through incarnations. The consumption patterns of a parent are picked up by the kids as easily as we pick up a flu that has infected the whole city. We start learning from our parents right from the womb. The wants, desires, cravings, longings and addictions of a pregnant woman are absorbed by the baby she is carrying, the way a sponge absorbs water. Then this greed is fueled by the market for which every kid, adult or an old person is just another potential customer. The market has nothing to gain from your spiritual liberation. It just wants you to desire, buy and consume. The more greedy you are, the greater your consumption; the greater your consumption, the more valuable you are for the market. There is a silent war that goes on between the stimuli of the world and your will to liberate yourself from all the clinging of the mind. It is this tussle that sponsors most of your anxiety.

Greed is not just limited to desires and consumptions; it has been described by our sages as the "Father of a sin". History has witnessed several times the relationship between a greed, a betrayal and a crucifixion. There is a story that goes like this. A king was once asked by another, "Who do you think is the father of sin?" The king said, "I'll let you know in a few days" and called a meeting of all his wise Brahmins. He gave the senior-most Brahmin two options – either to come up with an answer within a week or to get out of the kingdom. The Brahmin set out in search of the answer and could not solve the puzzle by the end of the fourth day. By now he was really worried. It was late evening and he was resting for a while under the shade of a tree – all tensed up. A Fakeer (Saint) who happened to be a farmer by profession, was looking after his goats a few yards away. He figured it all out with his spiritual powers and approached the worried Brahmin with a compassionate smile on his face. "What is it that troubles you my dear?" he asked. The Brahmin told him everything. "Don't worry, I have got the answer to that" he said. "But I will tell you on one condition". "What's that?" the Brahmin responded with enthusiasm. "You shall have to drink my goat's milk for that". Now, Brahmins don't drink goat's milk. So it took him some time to decide. "It's against my religion but if you say so I will do that", he said after some reluctance. The farmer milked one of his goats and held the bowl of milk in his hands. The Brahmin was eager to get over with it. "Wait a bit", the Fakeer said. "Let me have a few sips first". Now to feed on someone's left over is again considered irreligious by the Brahmins. So the Brahmin was once again fighting with his conscience. But the desire for the answer to the puzzle overpowered his morality and after some hesitation he agreed to drink from the Fakeer's bowl. "Just one last condition", the Fakeer said again. "I will pour the milk in my shoe and you will have to drink from that if you really want the answer". Now this was too much for the Brahmin. He had never ever felt that humiliated. But by now, his greed for the answer had grown out of proportion. So he threw away all shame and morality and reached out for the milk poured into the shoe by the Fakeer. As he was about to go for the most humiliating drink of his life, the Fakeer held his arm so that the shoe did not touch his lips and said, "Dear friend, you have already got your answer. The father of sin is greed". Greed can throw all of us in gutters of immorality.

All corruption and all extra marital affairs are because of greed. When a person is not satisfied with that which belongs to him, he wants to snatch that which belongs to others. Like a vampire, he starts feeding on the blood of others. The man of faith who is dwelling in love stops at necessities and some luxuries. After that he starts considering the necessities of others. But a man suffering from greed neither stops at necessities, nor at luxuries, not even at indulgence. He stops nowhere. He just cannot stop. He will snatch someone's luxuries for the sake of his indulgence and someone's necessities for the sake of his luxuries. He will crucify the other so that he can live longer. Greed is a fire that burns away all the virtues of a man and converts him into a selfish hungry being. It is the breeding ground of usurpers, traitors and tyrants. It was the greed for a throne that made many of the rulers kill their own real brothers and throw away their father inside a jail. It was greed that made unfaithful women poison and murder their own husbands and then sleep with someone else. It is greed that is nibbling the character of every citizen of our country and creating an environment which no one wants to live in.

There is a very uneasy feeling associated with greed and it surfaces when you stand in a shopping mall with tens of thousands of products displayed on the racks. Suddenly all these desires wake up in you and your soul turns so demanding. You may not have noticed it but every desire of ours is a mild torture for the soul. It reminds you that there is something inside you which can consume the whole town and still not be satisfied. There is a part of us that is tired of this ceaseless wanting and knows that nothing much is required to be happy and blissful. But it is too weak to occupy the throne of our being and make a declaration. The pool of desires produced by people surrounding us triggers our own greed and the mass effect soon converts an individual into a customer. Within minutes we find ourselves buying something or the other just to handle the momentum of our desires and when we step out of the exit gate, a sigh of relief comes from every atom of our being.

Greed makes us unavailable to the miraculous life that has been given to us free of cost. We are so occupied with how to get more that we have no time for that which we have already got. Desire has been described by the Buddha as the root of all misery. It robs us of the present moment and makes us victims of the dimension of time. When you want something and you don't have it, you obviously look towards the future for a fulfillment of your wish. But this splits the dimension of time into three parts – the past, present and future and distances you from the "Now". You are no longer in a "Yes Mode" regarding the present moment; you are in a conflict with it. This conflict is the root cause of all our misery. We are rarely happy because of what we have; most of the time, we are sad because of what we don't have. We think we need this to be happy and that to be abundant. But what we actually need is love and love does not require a future to manifest. The raw material required for its manifestation has always been with you all through. When you give and forgive, love manifests. You don't have to wait for anything to change in order to become worthy of love. The magic wands of giving and forgiving can manifest it for you.

The moment we look at someone's beautiful car, someone's beautiful house or someone's beautiful wife, the greed in us wants one for itself. The greatest amount of stimulus reaches our greed through our eyes. The rest of it enters in the form of sound, smell, taste and touch. When we walk through a city or town, our senses are being continuously bombarded with every kind of a stimulus and the spiritualist in us is continuously saying "No", "No", "No" to these nagging desires. The problem is not with the "No"; the problem is with the stimulus being able to stimulate. There must be something in us that it is able to excite. As long as it is there, it will keep on sponsoring all kinds of wants and keep on torturing us. So the secret lies in living in the thickness of the world of stimuli and extricating your being from it so gracefully that neither the world nor the being finds it harsh. This is what every sage means by renunciation.

The absence of greed, which has been called renunciation, also needs to be understood in order to understand greed. Renunciation does not mean hanging your desires by neck till death. It also does not mean running away from the stimuli of the world. These approaches have been tried and they have badly failed. Someone rightly said, "What you resist; persists"; whatever you run away from, starts chasing you. If you run away from the world or your desires, they will keep on haunting you. You have to live in this world and still be untouched by it, like a drop of oil in a bucket of water. The nature of the stimuli has to be known in depth. The nature of a desire has to be known in depth. That which all the desires come from has to be known. The satisfaction which comes from the fulfillment of a desire has to be known. A Buddha is not a man who has never had a desire; he is someone who has run around chasing objects of desire, watched the satisfaction fade away, new desires born out of the womb of greed and the meaninglessness of the whole pattern. The one who wakes up to the pattern of greed is sooner or later liberated from it once and for all. He can see the whole world moving from one desire to another in pursuit of a joy that can only come from standing still and waking up to the incessant wanting, craving and longing of our greed.

You may not be aware of it but there are things that you have renounced in life. You do not feel like doing them anymore and you do not derive any pleasure from doing them. It is not that you are struggling with yourself to "Not Do" them; they have simply fallen off your soul like a ripe fruit falls off the branch of a tree. When all your clinging falls off like that, you can call it renunciation. It is not that the tree is busy pushing its fruits away from itself and then lamenting over the separation; the fruits fall off due to their own ripening. To know the taste of renunciation we need to know how to assist our own greed in ripening. We have to allow it to mature and that can only be done by waking up to it and inviting love. Love makes it possible for you to witness the mortality of all satisfactions and the witnessing itself liberates you from the hold that desires exercise upon your soul. The "looking at them" creates a space between the stimuli of the world and your response to them. This space is the secret of your spiritual freedom and only a free soul can renounce anything.

A seed cannot bear a fruit. A seed grows into a tree and the tree bears fruit. Our spiritual practices are the seed, our understanding is the tree and renunciation is the fruit. Our goal should be to understand, to know. If we try to bypass an understanding and throw a desire out of the front door, it will enter our being from the back door. If we start fighting against our desires or start wrestling with them, our mind will become a Kurukshetra; a battlefield. A lot of our spiritual energy will be wasted in this tussle between two halves of our own self and it will most probably weaken us physically and mentally. We will evolve anyhow but at a very high cost. It would be a very unhealthy way of evolving. The ideal way or the healthy way would be to design our practices with emphasis on understanding our greed, not fighting it or wrestling with it.

You may have never given it a thought that our greatest greed is not for wealth, power, fame, sex and all the sensual pleasures; our greatest greed is for life itself. All the other "Greeds" add to it. They make our life invaluable. And it is. But what we need to understand is that its preciousness lies in living it and knowing it, not in clinging to it. In our clinging to it, it loses its glory. The extra-ordinary is reduced to ordinary when we try to freeze impermanence. In doing that, we are only able to exist and survive; we are not able to evolve and expand. The greed for life creates fear of losing it and because of this fear our consciousness is unable to expand. We fail to acknowledge that whatever has been given to us in this incarnation will be taken away at the time of our death and we will leave this plane of reality with nothing but our Karma and our wisdom, our knowing, our insights.

The greed for life can keep you away from the nucleus of religion and the nucleus of religion is the spot where Shri Krishna and Arjun are standing in the battle of Mahabharata. Religion is not just a few spiritual practices and an enlightenment; it can ask for all kinds of sacrifices. The ones we remember as Martyrs, were Saints who decided to offer their lives in order to save and protect religion. Those who have a very strong greed for life are unable to participate in revolutions and instead choose to watch the greatest of social events from a safe distance. But a liberation watched is not a liberation earned. Real freedom is not that which falls into the lap of worldly spectators; it is the one that becomes a part of the souls of freedom fighters. It is not something that can be earned by one and then passed on to another; everyone has to earn it for himself. The greed for life could prove to be the last obstacle to ultimate freedom. All that you can possibly cling to has to be consciously untangled and your relationship with the whole existence outside and inside you has to be revised so that it cannot create any suffering for you. The excess of suffering must be eliminated in order to make life livable. Life should not look or feel like a punishment or a sentence.

When you step out of the world and look back at it, greed appears in the form of a fire that is consuming the whole of mankind. You see the various ways in which it manifests itself and you see men and women dancing to the tune of their desires like puppets. It is consuming wisdom, knowledge, loyalties, ideals, intellect and all that can be considered supreme in a human incarnation. The individual is burning, the family is burning, the community is burning, the states and nations are burning. Everything seems to be on fire. Wherever you see, you see the flames of greed. Someone is offering food to the flames and overeating, someone is offering drugs to the flames and indulging in "Instant Nirvana", someone is offering sex to the flames and trying to explore that possibility to its limits, someone is offering power struggles to it, someone is offering fan following and fame to it; they are all offering something to the flames of greed and encouraging the fire. Rarely someone tries to extinguish it.

What possibly could a king do with a hundred queens? And we all know that a few centuries ago they had that many. Any honest married man knows that one woman is not only enough but more than enough to liberate your consciousness from the imprisonment of sexuality. One queen should have been enough for a king because he was also a man only and not a superman. But they needed 99 for their greed. In some way or the other we are all like those kings. We want one for our need and 99 for our greed. Be it money, land, wife or anything that fulfils some want of ours. We use one and offer 99 to the fire of desires. Unless and until we extinguish that fire, we cannot rise above the mass consciousness. We will be born into it, we will live in it and we will be consumed by it. The fire can only be extinguished by realizing that incessant desires are not something to be fulfilled; they are something to be risen above. When you have put out that fire, your requirements will be like leaves, flowers and fruits growing out of a tree, not like flames rising from a furnace.

Greed is one of the major forces that feed the ambitions of an ordinary man. Without an ego and without greed, the ambitions of an ordinary man cannot survive. These two engines keep him running all day. Whatever he does, he does to satisfy some desire of his. With such a frame of mind when he moves around, the whole existence is, for him, something to be exploited in order to make his dreams come true. Even when he comes across a Buddha, he will try to fit him into his plan of action. But an enlightened one is always "Un-exploitable." He is very acutely aware of how he spends himself on the rest of the mankind and would never ever offer the rein of his incarnation in the hands of an ignorant and selfish desirer.

For this very reason the people of the world find the Saint a bit frustrating. They wish to exploit and he refuses to be exploited. The ordinary man is charged with greed; the Buddha's energy field is that of compassion. Greed is just a small kid and compassion is like a father. The kid cannot fit a parent into his schemes; the parent always fulfills the kid's demands out of compassion.

Greed always makes you sell your principles in order to buy or earn the object of your desire. If we have two athletes preparing for the Olympian gold medal in 100 meters and the one who ultimately wins the race is found to have done it with the help of steroids, he has fallen prey to his greed. The prostitute is not the only one who sells her body, mind and soul due to greed; we all do that to some extent. When a singer sings a vulgar song or a model agrees to nudity, it is all done under the effect of greed. The ones who get it done from you are basically manipulating your greed to satisfy theirs. It is like a king cobra feeding on another snake. This is the basic molecule that goes into the making of this world; one greed manipulating the other. It's a deadly conspiracy that is responsible for all the corruption on earth. If you are beyond your greed, no one can lure you into the trap of immorality.

Just as our consciousness evolves from a thickness to a subtlety, our greed also transforms itself to merge into the consciousness. The greed of a businessman is simply for money and all that can be bought with it. In the politician, it manifests itself as a hunger for power and control. This is more subtle than the greed of a businessman. But in the so-called spiritualist, it becomes even more subtle and lurks in his immature spirituality like a serpent in the grass. He starts invading, conquering and ruling with his spiritual powers and becomes a "Local God". He judges and punishes others for their imperfections and gets so addicted to the thing that he totally forgets that he is also being watched by the laws of the universe. Greed incorporates violence in your way of living. The businessman is violent in his business, the politician is violent in his politics and the so-called spiritualist is violent in his spirituality. As long as your being does not give birth to compassion, greed goes on affecting the color of your soul.

To the worldly man, the absence of greed appears to be laziness, lethargy and lack of entrepreneurship. When we do not know something, we try to label it according to our own understanding instead of admitting our spiritual handicap. When people come in touch with an enlightened being, they never say, "He is beyond my comprehension or he belongs to a space I have not touched yet"; they always try to translate him into that which they know. It is like describing the moon by standing on the surface of the earth. In the absence of greed, your desire becomes the desire of God because in your thought the existence sees the good of all and that is the most basic nature of existence – "The good of all". The enlightened also do everything that an ordinary man does but there is no selfish lust in their Karma. Their karma is as pure as nectar and their achievements are as natural as the blossoming of a flower. There is no aggression in their progress and no plundering in their profits. Everything is divine.

Because of greed, our markets are very aggressive and violent. There is an old saying, "The butcher cuts the throat while the salesman cuts the pocket". The moment you enter a showroom, you feel as if someone is trying to push his hand inside your pocket and reach out for your purse. The vibrations seem to be robbing you of your hard earned money. You may have just dropped in to have a look at the products offered by the brand but you can hear a whisper that says, "You cannot walk in and out of this place without buying something. This is not a park; this is a showroom." A Mantra is being recited by everyone in his or her subconscious mind, "Money", "Money", "Money", "Money" and you can sense it. It is not without any reason that the environment inside a showroom is so suffocating for us. Greed always tries to stuff itself by robbing the other. The only question is whether that robbing is simple or sophisticated.

When a person who has risen above greed sells a product or a service, there is no aggression in his selling. He will not try to push you into making a decision; though he may help you in making one. Your wellbeing will be primary for him and his sales will be secondary. His mind will not be focused on making sales; it will be focused on the satisfaction of customers and the purity of his own karma. Beyond greed, there is a religiousness in the equation which has got the service you offer on the left and the money you make on the right. There is no manipulation and politics in the equation. Everything is simple and clear. The greedy always try to separate their business from their religion. They worship their God and exploit fellow human beings. But the one who has extinguished that fire sees every human being as God in disguise and tries to make every interaction with others religious. The fragrance of the truth, "Religion is what a religious man does", emanates from his Karma.

What we need to understand is that greed does not bring abundance into our life; it rather cuts us off from the real abundance. To the world we may appear to be growing and expanding but deep within, we go on shrinking. A hundred wives do not make you 100 times more manly than the common man and a 100 billion annual turnover does not make you that many times happier than the common man. Greed believes in quantity and the greatest mysteries of life are found in quality; not quantity. There is nothing in a Saint that is X times a common man; he simply belongs to a different dimension, a different realm of reality. But the fire of desires can keep us stuck in quantities and magnitudes. We would either like to have something more than what we already have or something bigger than what we already have. We will be unable to comprehend the nature of things like love, compassion and enlightenment which are not more or bigger but simply different than what we have experienced so far. This shift from quantity to quality is very essential for realizing your true potential.

Imagine a king who steps out of his palace one day and is somehow unable to remember that he is a king. He walks around the city begging for his bare necessities and mere survival. He spends days, months and years trying to make the ends meet till someone from the palace recognizes him as the king. The moment he steps into the palace he comes back to his senses and remembers all that he had forgotten. We are all like this king. When we allow our being to be overpowered by greed and step out of the palace of our soul, we get lost in the world of consumption. We spend years running around trying to satisfy our desires and hoping for a way to happiness or some secret of fulfillment. Then one day someone who has discovered real joy spots us in the crowd and introduces us to the science of spirituality. Contrary to the popular belief, we soon find that joy is not in offering things to the fire of desires but in the extinguishing of it with meditation, self control and all the spiritual practices which assist us in leading a truly pious life.

Greed is like a wandering of the mind and love is like coming back home. Our mind is basically a wanderer. Now it is here, now it is in Germany, then in Russia, then again back to a pain in our body and back to Germany. Since the mind has a great role to play in the making up of greed, greed takes us away from our home which - is pure consciousness. Our senses pull us out of our solace and the mouthwatering temptations of the world continue to stimulate our greed and make it respond to them with desire after desire. Greed, in other words, is a factory of desires. There are those that ask for an immediate gratification, there are those that need some time to fulfill and there are those that can never be fulfilled. We call them fantasies. Greed knows no limits. It starts pouring out of the vessel of practicality when we do not do something about it. The desires of most of us are overflowing. They are so many that our consciousness finds it difficult holding them inside. This excess is one of the major sources of our stress; our anxiety.

Now, the anxiety of the intellectual is different from that of the businessman and the anxiety of the spiritualist is different from that of the intellectual. The most subtle of all the desires is the desire to be desire-less. As Acharya Rajneesh puts it, "Nirvana is the last nightmare". The greed for enlightenment can be just as torturing as the greed for money or the greed for sex. In life, every atom is a paradox. You can detach yourself from everything and then get attached to detachment itself. Shri Ram Dass says that one of the greatest insights is the one that there is nowhere to stand. When "Desireless-ness" becomes an obsession, you start looking at your desires as if they were your enemies and start battling with them. This converts your soul into a battlefield with one half of yours fighting against the other half. This duality can produce a very high amount of stress and then give birth to all the stress related ailments in the body as well as in the mind. It makes a spiritual practitioner bitter and in a very subtle way violent also. Desires are to be witnessed, not shot to death or hanged by neck and "Desireless-ness" is not to be desired; it is to be allowed as the natural next thing. When the clouds of greed disappear with your gaze, the pure, clear sky of your being shows up. There is no need to desire, seek or practice very hard for enlightenment; it is the natural next thing in the process of witnessing. The fact is that if you keep on watching, you cannot stop enlightenment from happening.

From the desire of enlightenment, another desire is born; the desire to be with the enlightened. Being with them appears to us as a ticket to Nirvana or a shortcut to the "Kingdom of god." But the Saint only acts as a catalyst; your spiritual journey has to be made by you. The best reason for being with a Saint would be love and it is very rare. Most of us approach them with some greed inside; it could be this, it could be that. There is something we have been striving for and the Saint has got it. This greed of ours can make the Saint feel as if we are using him like a stepping stone. He is not a stone; he is a flower of awareness and love is the fragrance that emanates from him. But to be touched by that fragrance, we have to be available to it. No fixed models; no greed. Both these things will make you unavailable to him. The Saint is like the present moment; unless you are totally there, you will miss his essence.

Our greed always makes us unavailable to life and ungrateful to God. Our desire for the one thing that we don't have sucks up all the joy that we can derive from the 99 we have. That "One short of hundred" becomes our suffering. So, most of the time, we are just one or two desires away from happiness. Our want becomes the resistance between us and the existence. We start behaving like God's nagging wife. To the universe our soul does not appear in the form of a flower of consciousness; it appears in the form of a cloud of demands or a part of the existence at war with the rest of it. The healing of greed with witnessing and love heals the resistance between us and the rest of the creation. From a bundle of unfulfilled desires, we become a flower of understanding and acceptance. The nature of our being and the nature of spiritual practice is such that whatever we come to understand, stops bothering us. Desires bother us only as long as we have not found their origin and understood it. The root cause has to be found and cured.

Anything that separates us from the divine will is a cause of our suffering. The desire of God cannot be seen through the prism of our greed. We tend to dye the existence in the color of our desires. The bachelor sees women, the poor sees richness, the prisoner sees freedom, the sick sees health, the hungry sees food and the miserable sees happiness. We impose our desire upon the existence and become deaf and numb to the divine will. The whisper of God gets lost in the noise of our desires and the violence of thoughts injures our mind. Meditation and witnessing or mindful watching helps us in silencing our mind and dispelling our greed. In this silence we are able to hear the voice of the Supreme Being. And when we are able to trust that voice, we are able to understand what Jesus meant by, "Not my will but thy will be done". From slaves of desire we evolve into instruments of peace, love, compassion and freedom.

As long as we are driven by our desires, we will keep on creating thick Karmic stuff for ourselves; the very thing that has sponsored most of our pain. In order to eliminate one pain, we will be unknowingly creating another one. Greed makes our Karma impure. It makes us selfish and sometimes even inhumane. Our desires are only the branches and leaves; the root is always greed and as long as we are pouring violence into the roots, the leaves, branches and fruit cannot be those of compassion. The emptiness of greed ought to be filled with meditation, mindfulness, witnessing and awareness; it is not to be stuffed with the gratification of violent desires. Our desires are rarely in harmony with the rest of the existence; most of them are violent. We try to break and bend the rules of the existence in order to get what we want. We try to use every atom of the existence as a stepping stone and all this creates a lot of Karmic stuff. We keep on sowing a crop that we would not like to reap.

On one hand we have the world of temptations; foods of all kinds for our various hungers. On the other hand we have this well of greed inside us, the well without a bottom and these two are connected through our senses. Now if we don't do something about this equation, it is a hopeless situation; a trap. It would be like offering ourselves to be consumed by our greed, our senses and the temptations of the world. This is what makes Moksh essential for anyone who wishes to be liberated from the equation I just mentioned. We cannot reduce the world to zero, we cannot kill our senses. All that we can do is, withdraw ourselves from all of them and seek refuge in a space or dimension that is neither the hunger nor the fulfillment which comes from feeding ourselves on the food of our desire. This space, this dimension is our only hope.

I will try to explain this with the most common desire, the sexual desire. When a man looks at the picture of a nude woman, the picture serves the purpose of food. His eyes are the senses through which he is feeding his lust and the vibrations of lust produced in his being are his gratification. But there is something, which if withdrawn, can change the whole situation. The hunger will subside, the waves of lust will fall back into the ocean of your infinity and your eyes will be reduced to a lens and a retina. This something is your supreme self. It is the door that opens into Moksh. The beauty of a human incarnation is that we have the choice to withdraw ourselves from all our instincts and refuse to entertain our desires. Animals can't do that. The potential of Moksh is only available to us and if there is any real golden opportunity on earth, then this is it.

The pleasures of life are not free of cost; each and every one of them is accompanied by an equal amount of pain. It is this pain that makes it necessary to step away from greed. For any true spiritual practitioner, Moksh is not a luxury, it is his necessity, for the simple reason that to pull someone out of a well you have to be out of the well yourself. Otherwise, how can you pull? The suffering that comes with the very nature of desires is what provides all the meaning to liberation from them. The ones who got enlightened got enlightened in the process of eliminating suffering from their incarnation. We have a very faint idea of what we are walking towards but we are absolutely clear about what we wish to walk away from. Our suffering is very tangible. There is no doubt about it and once you wake up to the pain of desires, you cannot ignore it. You can pretend to sleep but you won't be able to sleep. You won't be able to unlearn what you have learnt and what you have learnt is this – With every worldly pleasure comes an equal amount of pain.

It is not possible to throw away the pain without throwing away the pleasure and this is where the whole world gets stuck. To some extent, everyone knows this and the problem that arises is, "What will someone be left with if he throws away all that he has got?". We are greedy because we do not know any other way of being. The key for this lock is meditation. Meditation introduces you to the dimension that is beyond the reach of both pleasure and pain. This dimension makes it possible for you to stand at a distance from your desires and wake up to their fundamental make up. Once you have understood greed, it looks like a foolishness. But without the space created by meditation, it would not have been possible for you to study your inside. You could never have known the threads that run through your incarnations; the software in your body. Meditation separates you from your consumptions and the separation makes it possible for you to decide what to consume and how much. Without this control, liberation would have been impossible. Moksh was discovered by souls tortured by their incessant desiring.

When you are possessed by your desires, the pleasures of the senses, the hungers and gratifications seem to be the essence of life. The smells, sounds, scenes, tastes and touches appear to be the very meaning of life. The orgasm is your climax of joy. But when you wake up to the mortality of all this, it looks like the wastage of an incarnation. It turns out to be the very thing that is holding you back from realizing your true potential. It is like a Mr. Olympia contestant becoming aware of his eating habits and all his weak points. Meditation provides strength to the witness in you and expands the space required for your refuge. It makes it possible for you to exist in a way where you are neither the hunger nor the gratification; neither the pain nor the pleasure, neither the desire nor the desirer. With your gaze, it all collapses.

As your greed starts fading out, all the "More of this" and "More of that" are reduced to "Just one more this" and "Just one more that". To the consumer in you is added the witness and that means you are not only aware of a desire, you are also aware of the emptiness it is incapable of filling. This simultaneous sprouting of two different kinds of energies is a bit challenging in the beginning but it is inevitable because this is the only way of realizing what it is that stands between the you that you are and the you that you wish to be. The Buddha in you seems within your reach and all your basic instincts are something of the past. You don't want to postpone your bloom and everything other than the peace within, feels like an addiction you need to quit. It is as if you are standing at the doorstep with one foot in the world and the other in Nirvana. You can feel the chains of habits more than ever before and your whole being seems to be waiting anxiously for the silence within to explode.

The man who has risen above greed cannot be comprehended by the world. As Shri Ram Dass puts it, "He simply does not feel like eating and the world thinks he is fasting." Some fine day, you will find yourself facing a situation similar to that and when you do, you must accept not being able to explain everything to everyone as a part of the way things are. The beauty of some things lies in their unexplainable characteristics. The world will keep on desiring and consuming but you won't belong to it anymore. When you have a diamond worth billions in your pocket, why would you care for cheaper stuff? With a heart full of compassion, who cares for all the worldly consumptions? Your desire for things will be replaced by the urge to give, share and distribute. It will be so overwhelming that you will often forget what belongs to you and what belongs to the other. You will see yourself in the other and the other in you. Your individual needs and your personal suffering will be dissolved in a pool of compassion for the needs and suffering of others and from a slave of desires you will grow into a man of cause. In your mere presence, needs will be fulfilled and suffering eliminated.

About The Author

Shri Charanjit Singh was born in the Patiala district of Punjab, in village Dhenthal, on the 30th of April 1972. His father, Shri Kulwant Singh, served as a senior auditor in the cooperative bank and his mother Swarn Kaur was a simple housewife. Shri Saudagar Singh, the author's grandfather, was a hard core meditator and a man of Truth and it was most probably, his occasional company in the initial years that introduced the author's soul to the taste of Bhakti or devotion. In 1972, Shri Kulwant Singh got transferred to the Sangrur district and so the whole family shifted to this town. Along with his elder brother Manjit Singh, who later joined the Indian Army and is now serving as a P.C.S. officer, this kid studied from nursery to the fifth standard in General Gurnam Singh Public School Sangrur. In 1979, this family was blessed with another baby boy Harjit Singh who is now an upcoming popstar living in Sydney (Australia). The author has some beautiful memories of this first decade of his incarnation and the word Sangrur means to him a lot more than just the name of another town. In 1983 Shri kulwant Singh got posted back to Patiala and the younger two kids got admitted in Yadavindra Public School Patiala(Y.P.S.). Elder brother Manjit went to Sainik School Kapurthala. From the sixth to the twelvth standard, the author studied here. The family started living at the village which was approximately 22 Kilometers from school and stayed here for the next 19 years.

These were the years when the province of Punjab was going through a very violent change. The environment of the village was also not healthy for a soul as sensitive as that of the author. Both these factors had a very profound effect on the consciousness of this young boy and his inner world went through a metamorphosis. This was his initiation into the quest for meaning and though after passing out from the school in 1990, he became an engineering student but the inner turmoil did not let him concentrate on his studies and after quitting in the third year of his degree, he started taking formal training in classical as well as western music from two different institutes in Pune. Music provided his aimless life with a meaning and a purpose and it also took care of his spiritual restlessness. The notes and beats made more sense than the assignments back in the engineering college.

During the transition from saying goodbye to a full fledged career in engineering to pursuing his passion of music, Shri Charanjit Singh came in contact with the spiritual mentor of the Namdhari sect of Sikhs, Satguru Jagjit Singh Ji and he firmly believes that this power is protecting and guiding him even today. Shri Charanjit Singh has no doubt regarding the difference that Guru Kripa makes in the life of a Shishya, a disciple. From his own experience, he knows that all which is praiseworthy in him and his personal world is not just a result of his own efforts; much of it is his Guru's blessings.

Along with music, Shri Charanjit Singh became deeply interested in the various meditation techniques, especially the ones designed by Acharya Rajneesh and being practiced at the Ashram in Koregaon Park Pune. The potential of these techniques, in liberating an individual from the prison of the mind and the suffering it creates, held great promise for this young revolutionary who was looking for ways to deal with the pain that is inherent in a human incarnation. With the purification of his soul and the evolution of his consciousness, Shri Charanjit Singh became increasingly aware of the part or role he played in the unfolding of life and his responsibility as a conscious being with regard to the degradation of human values and corruption of all kinds on such a large scale, in the environment, of which, he was an integral part. He realized that the glory of wisdom is in it being able to serve mankind by illuminating the lives of fellow beings with compassion and consciousness. This book is also an expression of his concern for the whole of mankind and the realization of his own duty. Through words, he is encouraging each and every one of us to establish religiousness inside and around us since that is the only way to make this earth livable.

Any religious person has got basically three means to share his vision, his perception with the rest – books, audio/video recordings and personal contact. There was an era when personal contact was the only option available. All the three modes have got their benefits and limitations. For example, the way you can go into the details and intricacies of an issue in a book, is not possible in a chance conversation. But the shared awareness that comes into being in a conversation and the resonance of vibrations that manifests through a personal meeting of compatible souls, cannot be expected from the reading of a book or the listening of an audio recording. Shri Charanjit Singh is also making an honest attempt in using the mediums available to him to reach out to sincere souls like you. If a welfare organization feels the need of the service he has to offer, he tries his best to live up to their expectations. Wherever he is felt needed, he gives 1-2 hr. talks on the topics of addiction, Dharma, Karma, spiritual freedom and meditation. In every possible way, he tries to help as well as serve the rest of us, knowing well his limitation and capacity as a human being.

Moksh Publications

Moksh
PUBLICATIONS

www.ingramcontent.com/pod-product-compliance
Lightning Source LLC
Chambersburg PA
CBHW021125020426
42331CB00005B/635